THIS BOOK IS DEDICATED TO THE CLASSROOM TEACHER

Teach and Retire Rich

by Dan Otter

This publication is designed to provide accurate and authoritative information in regard to the subject matter covered. It is published with the understanding that the publisher and author are not engaged in rendering legal, accounting, or other professional service. If legal advice or other professional advice, including financial, is required, the services of a competent professional person should be sought.
— from a *Declaration of Principles, jointly adopted by a Committee of the American Bar Association and a Committee of Publishers*

All charts in this book are presented for illustrative purposes only and do not reflect actual performance, or predict future results, of any investment account.

ISBN 0-9726117-1-1

Teach and Retire Rich

WILLIAM J. BERNSTEIN, Ph.D., M.D.

Foreward

A good deed never goes unpunished. You scrimped and saved to get your college degree and teaching certificate. You endured the inanities of the public school bureaucracy, threadbare educational budgets, demanding parents, rapidly shrinking health care coverage, and salaries that would not be envied by a twenty-something assistant manager at McDonald's.

But the crowning insult is the retirement plan you are saddled with: the 403(b). If your 403(b) looks like most, it's larded with fees and expenses that will slowly leach your retirement assets over the decades and contains nowhere near enough diversification to properly control risk. Worst of all, you are the investment genius who has to see things through. That's because most schools have ceded responsibility for the 403(b) to you, the individual. It's as if they bumped you from your flight to Cleveland on a Boeing 777 into a Piper Cub. And no one thought to give you flying lessons.

Teach and Retire Rich is your map of and survival guide to the financial heart of darkness you've been parachuted into. You'll learn the lay of the land, the combat strategies you'll need to survive, what the predators look like, and, most importantly, how to stay as far away as possible from them.

How much do you need to retire? When can you retire? How does a pension work? What is a 457(b)? What funds should you buy? As Dan will explain, that's duck soup. The hard part is mustering the discipline and nerve to see the thing through.

Like dieting or quitting smoking, the planning is easy; it's the execution that causes problems.

It is also important to know about something called "market efficiency"—the concept that although some investors outperform others, this apparent superiority is due to luck, not skill. This profound insight has earth-shaking implications for small investors like yourself:

- Superior mutual fund returns usually do not persist; making your fund selections on the basis of prior performance is a fool's errand.

- Since performance cannot be predicted, one thing, and one thing only, matters: expenses. And mark me well—the typical 403(b) plan contains some of the most egregiously expensive fund choices in the entire universe of investing. Getting the least expensive and most efficient fund vehicles into your portfolio will involve not just choosing the pick of the litter from your plan's list; you may have to educate and lobby your union and school administration to get a decent selection.

You will not be able to avoid learning a little bit about financial theory—the essential relationship between risk and return, why markets are unpredictable, and what it means for your retirement. Dan will make this as painless as possible, and who knows, once you understand how the markets work, you may actually begin to enjoy the process.

You can retire rich, but it will require knowledge, discipline, and, yes, not a little luck. Successful investing is a lifelong journey; let Dan provide you with your roadmap and travel kit.

WILLIAM J. BERNSTEIN, Ph.D., M.D., a neurologist and best-selling author of investment books such as *The Four Pillars of Investing* and, most recently, *The Birth of Plenty*, likes to joke that "investing isn't brain surgery." One of the most respected financial thinkers and writers of our time, he counts Vanguard founder John C. Bogle as an admirer. To learn more about Mr. Bernstein, visit *www.efficientfrontier.com.*

CHAPTER ONE

Intrinsic Riches

"A wise man should have money in his head, but not in his heart."
— Jonathan Swift

I have held several jobs since I graduated from San Diego State University in 1988—journalist, elementary school teacher, middle school teacher, website owner, and college professor. Without a doubt, the most difficult job I have ever held was that of an elementary and middle school teacher. Teaching children is exhausting. The kids can be exhausting. The bureaucracy can be exhausting. And the constant public debate on public education can be exhausting. I have always found it curious that so many people purport to be experts on education, yet so few of these so-called experts have actually spent time in the classroom teaching. While mostly well-intentioned, national and state "top-down" management of education has had a smothering effect on the most critical ingredient in teaching: the teacher. I have lost count of the number of colleagues who have left the profession recently. They grew tired of the lack of support, tired of the new testing mandates, tired of the relatively low pay. Nationwide, teachers are leaving the education profession at an alarming clip. Consider the following figures from the National Center for Education Statistics and the National Education Association:

- Six percent of the nation's teaching force leaves the profession every year.

- Twenty percent of all new hires leave teaching within three years.
- More than half of all new teachers leave the profession in their first five years.
- Some two million teachers will be needed nationwide by 2008–09 as a result of teacher attrition, teacher retirement, and increased student enrollment.

This book is in part an effort to help stop teacher attrition and to recruit new talent into the profession. It is also an effort to alert teachers to powerful wealth-building tools at their disposal. But that is not the whole story. Money should never be the focus of a career choice. I urge all teachers and those considering the profession to also focus on the intrinsic riches of teaching. As a talented former colleague of mine, sixth-grade teacher George Corwin of Corona, California, is fond of saying: "When things go well in private-sector work, the feeling is good. But when things go well in the classroom, the feeling is great. It cannot be matched."

At some point we all depart this earth. What kind of legacy do we plan to leave? Teaching affords us a wonderful opportunity to have a positive impact on the lives of children and on society. In 2001, I had the hideous misfortune of watching my wife, Julie, a teacher, pass away from breast cancer. As Julie's condition worsened, I thanked God that she was a teacher. I thanked God for the impact she had on so many students—many of whom contacted us when she was ill. I thanked God for the balanced life we led—decent compensation, time for family and travel, positive impact on others. I also thanked God for bringing this truly special "teacher" into my life. When you are looking at the bottom line as it relates to teaching, do not forget to factor in the true bottom line: time with family and a positive impact on others. Teaching affords the opportunity to do all of this and more.

WARM-UP ACTIVITY

You can't spell "knowledge" without the letters "KWL"

One of my favorite teaching strategies is the KWL activity. Here is how it works:

1. Before beginning a new unit, lesson, or activity, it is important to activate prior knowledge by asking and recording what students already know about a topic. This is the "K" in KWL.
2. Next ask students what they want to learn about the topic. This is the "W" in KWL. Again, record their responses.
3. Following the unit, lesson, or activity, revisit the K and W responses.
4. Now ask students what they did learn. This is the "L" in KWL. Record their answers.

I encourage you to engage in your own KWL activity with this book. What do you *know* about wealth building? What do you *want* to learn about wealth building? And finally, when you have finished reading this book, ask yourself what you have *learned* about wealth building. Record your answers on a piece of paper.

CHAPTER TWO

Teach and Retire Rich

"America believes in education: the average professor earns more money in a year than a professional athlete earns in a whole week."
— Evan Esar

Teach and retire rich? That sounds like a statement straight from the Oxymoron Hall of Fame. After all, the average teacher's salary in 2004, according to the NEA, was approximately $46,800. But what is your definition of rich? If it is to accumulate gobs of money and possessions and live in a McMansion, then chances are teaching will not allow you to retire rich. If, however, your definition of rich is to influence the lives and development of hundreds—perhaps thousands—of children and adults, and in exchange receive decent compensation with access to several powerful wealth-building tools, then teaching and retiring rich will be a very attainable goal.

Just as no student should be judged solely on the basis of standardized test scores, neither should the lifetime earning potential of teachers be based purely on average salary. Contrary to popular belief—and unknown to many teachers themselves—educators in this country have access to some very powerful wealth-accumulation tools. Most teachers are eligible for a defined-benefit plan, also known as a pension, that will provide a steady income in retirement. Many teachers are also eligible to receive Social Security (special rules and provisions regarding the collection of Social Security and a pension are discussed in Chapter Fourteen). Furthermore, teachers can contribute to not one, but two, 401(k)-style tax-deferred retirement plans: the 403(b) and the 457(b). Toss in a Roth IRA (available to all investors who meet certain income provisions), and teachers who plan accordingly could find themselves living a very comfortable retirement. All of these plans are explained in Chapter Five. It is not unusual for educators to accumulate hundreds of thousands of dollars, and in some cases millions of dollars, over time. The emphasis is on the word time. The strategies outlined in this book require discipline and a long-term view of investing. This book could just as easily be called *Teach and Grow Rich Slowly*. The earlier you begin saving, the longer and more attractive the view will be. This is not to say that teachers only ten years from retirement cannot accumulate a respectable retirement sum. They can, but they must begin saving today.

A word on retirement plans: the overwhelming majority of K–12 public school teachers and administrators (as well as many college and university professors) have access to both a pension plan and at least one tax-deferred retirement plan. The formula for financial success outlined in this book is:

> Pension plan and/or Social Security + 403(b) and/or 457(b) and/or Roth IRA retirement plan(s) allocated wisely over time = healthy retirement

Bear in mind, however, that not all employers offer all of these plans (NOTE: the Roth IRA is not an employer-sponsored plan). For those at institutions lacking either or all of these tools, you have two choices. First and foremost, lobby your employer to add these plans. Explain their value in helping to recruit and retain teachers. While you may be able to add a 403(b) and/or a 457(b) plan, you will most likely not be able to add a pension plan. These are enormously costly plans. In fact, as this book went to print, California was considering eliminating its two pension plans and replacing them with a 401(k)-style plan. If such a scenario becomes reality, the lessons in this book become even more important as teachers would then be responsible for making all of their own retirement plan decisions.

NOTE: While the financial strategies outlined in this book focus on educators, most of the approaches are directly applicable to all school employees—and, indeed, all workers. Unfortunately, defined-benefit (pension) plans are typically not available to school support personnel. This means that they have to be even more diligent about taking advantage of other available investment plans.

CHAPTER THREE

Living Proof

"The actual proves the possible." — Immanuel Kant

LYNDA
Retired rich

I spoke with newly retired Maryland middle school teacher Lynda
after most of this book was written. Thirty seconds into our
conversation, I realized that she is truly the one who wrote the
book on teaching and retiring rich. Not only did Lynda, age 57,
find teaching to be an enormously gratifying profession, but the
profession has also been enormously rewarding to her financially.
Consider: Lynda retired in June 2004, after a thirty-five-year
career as an elementary and middle school teacher, and now
draws an inflation-adjusted pension of $62,000 a year for life. She
has amassed more than $300,000 in two 403(b) accounts and will
receive full medical benefits for life. This latter benefit is of great
comfort to her—her husband was diagnosed with a rare form of
leukemia two years ago. He is doing well now, but the future is
fraught with uncertainty.

   "I tell teachers every chance I get that they have to start
saving now," Lynda says. "I didn't start a 403(b) until 1984. If
I had started my first day, it would have been worth a whole lot
more!"

   When Lynda first started her 403(b), she invested in a
fixed annuity. In 1994, a friend whose husband worked for Alan

Greenspan, the current chairman of the Federal Reserve, told her that she needed to be in no-load mutual funds. Lynda took this advice and is glad she did. She stopped contributing to the fixed annuity (which she still has) and directed all new money to a T. Rowe Price mutual fund. And she is glad she did not cash out of the annuity. "The annuity provided safety. The mutual fund has done very well and the fees are very low."

Lynda began contributing just $50 a month to her 403(b) in 1984. She increased this amount every year. Eventually she was contributing the maximum. "I never missed the money," she says. "It came out of my paycheck, so I just concentrated on what I had left. That was what I had to spend."

Along the way, Lynda went through a divorce in the mid-1980s. "I had to learn to manage money myself," she says. What is ironic is that her ex-husband was not very supportive of her decision to start a 403(b). "He thought it was stupid. But I was the little tortoise. He was the hare. I'm probably doing better than he is now."

While retirement excites Lynda, she is not exactly sure what she will do next (though she plans to do a lot of traveling). "I am looking forward to having time," she says. "I used to be able to teach and engage in hobbies and other interests. But the past several years I had so much responsibility at school." In addition to being the head of the World Studies department, she was a grade-level team leader. While the additional duties took extra time, they boosted her final year's salary to nearly $100,000 and helped increase the retirement formula for her pension. Maryland changed its pension retirement formula about a decade ago. For a mere $350, Lynda opted to remain part of the old system. This decision may have been her wisest, and has resulted in a pension that is worth thousands of dollars more each year than a pension under the new system. "I feel for the new teachers," she says. "They won't have as generous a payout. But that's another reason they need to start a 403(b)."

Lynda also advises K 12 public school teachers to earn as many graduate credits as possible. Public school teachers are paid on a salary schedule that rewards years of service and education enhancements such as master's degrees and PhDs—both of which Lynda earned. "I remember my first year of teaching how a colleague ten years my senior earned much more," Lynda says. "We both worked just as hard, but she earned more. I knew I couldn't make up the ten years on her, but I could earn more by taking more classes. I did this just about every year."

What will Lynda miss most about teaching? "When their eyes look at you and say, 'Aha! I get it!' You know learning is taking place. I just loved that. And it happened a lot." Here is hoping those reading Lynda's story have the same reaction.

JOE
Still working but well on his way

If Lynda is the poster child for the *Teach and Retire Rich* concept, 58-year-old Los Angeles elementary teacher Joe is well on his way to joining her. Joe, who is in his twentieth-eighth year of teaching elementary school in southern California, credits a former principal for setting him on the path to retiring rich twenty years ago. "He convinced me to start a 403(b)," Joe recalls. It was good advice. Joe's balance today stands at more than $250,000. He contributes the maximum each year to his 403(b). Additionally, Joe began fully funding a Roth IRA in 1998.

While Joe does not have a firm date for retirement in mind, he does not want to experience a drop in income when he does retire. "I plan to keep teaching until the amount I receive from CalSTRS [his pension] matches what I receive in my paycheck now," he says. Currently, 8% of Joe's salary goes to CalSTRS and 17% goes to his 403(b). This leaves him approximately 75% of his annual salary, or $45,000.

As it now stands, Joe's school district pays for health benefits for retirees. This may change, however, as health care costs continue to escalate. "This is not a happy thought," Joe says of the possibility of having health benefits rescinded when he retires.

Joe does not use an agent or advisor, but he has read a number of financial books. His favorites are those by Frank Anderson, William Bernstein, John C. Bogle, and Larry Swedroe. The current allocation of his portfolio—403(b) and Roth IRA plans—is 5% cash, 35% bonds, and 60% equities. He is gradually increasing his fixed investment holdings (cash and bonds) as his yet-unknown retirement date draws nearer.

Joe has the following advice for the young teacher:

A teacher who is starting out needs to begin saving right away with a 403(b)—and a Roth IRA if possible. Time and compounding are the friends of the beginning teacher. You can begin funding a 403(b) with a small amount of money, and increase it each time you get a pay increase. Keep part of the pay increase for yourself, and give part of it to the 403(b). This is a great way to fund a 403(b).

Joe has the following advice for the veteran teacher:

I think that veteran teachers should also consider funding both a 403(b) and a Roth IRA. It is not too late to begin doing something. It is doubtful that any teacher, young or veteran, will regret having saved some extra money for retirement; however, I can easily imagine someone wishing that they had put away a little more.

CHERYL
First-year teacher already reaping the intrinsic rewards

While Lynda and Joe are focused on the retirement years, 24-year-old kindergarten teacher Cheryl has just completed her first year of teaching. "It has been exhausting, stressful, and nonstop, but I have loved every minute and aspect of it," she says.

For Cheryl, saving for a retirement that is decades away takes a backseat to today's pressing monetary realities. "I do think about retirement, but with so many immediate issues in my life (insurance, house, school), it is so hard to find time and energy to sit down and plan for something that is so far off." While Cheryl does participate in her state's pension plan for teachers, she has yet to start a 403(b). "I can see it getting pushed back again because I haven't looked into it yet," she says.

While Cheryl has yet to begin fully participating in the monetary rewards of the profession, she has already been intrinsically enriched. She loves to see "the light bulb go on" in a student after days or even months of struggling with a concept. It has also been immensely rewarding to see the progress of her students. "Looking at beginning writing is amazing—to see how the students were writing at the beginning of the year and what they are doing now," Cheryl says. "It is great to think that I helped with that."

The biggest reward of all has been her students' progress in reading. "To me, literacy is such an amazing ability and privilege," Cheryl says. "Who else at retirement can say that they accomplished something as great as giving the gift and the love of literacy to hundreds of people?"

MARC
Late career changer who took a 75% pay cut to teach

As the director of clinical nutrition research for a major pharmaceutical company, Marc, 56, seemingly had it all. "It was a highly rewarding career from the standpoint of personal achievement, fulfillment as a scientist, satisfaction of having made a meaningful contribution to society, and of course, financial compensation," recalls Marc, who traded it all in the summer of 2003 to become a high school science teacher at a quarter of his previous salary.

Several factors contributed to the career- and life-changing decision, including the death of his mother. "It made me realize that a fast-paced, well-compensated, high-visibility career is of little value compared to the rewards of being with family," said Marc.

Also factoring into Marc's decision was geography. While his well-paid pharmaceutical company position was in the Midwest, his heart was in the small mountain town of Durango, Colorado. Not only did he love the beautiful, outdoor-oriented community, but his daughter and son-in-law, whom he counts as his two closest friends, live in the town. In no time, the decision to relocate with Sher, his wife of twenty-five years, became obvious.

Many years ago, before earning a doctorate in nutritional biochemistry, Marc had spent two years teaching high school in Chicago and St. Louis. "I was enthusiastic and idealistic, but young, immature, and inexperienced," Marc recalls. "After the second year, the opportunity to tour Europe and the Middle East on motorcycle and live in Israel with a college buddy was just too enticing for me to pass up."

Today, Marc is still idealistic enough to believe that teaching is a noble profession and that turning high school students on to science is of value to both the students and the community. "When I made the decision to leave industry, returning to my former career as a high school science teacher seemed to be an obvious choice."

The first year back in the classroom was more than a challenge for Marc—especially since he was hired only two days before the start of the school year. "Just as one doesn't really remember the feeling of pain, neither can one remember the acute angst of realizing that you are 'on' from the moment the bell rings to start the first period until the final bell of the day. No breaks."

Marc can say without hesitation that he has never been happier. "Admittedly, a great deal of my happiness is because my career change was accompanied by a move to be with my family in a wonderful location. But that's also part of the beauty of teaching. There are few places in the country that aren't in need of mature, motivated, and life-experienced individuals willing to work (and I do mean work) as a teacher."

Marc, who has started a 403(b), readily admits that financial management is not his strong suit. "I am probably one of the people targeted for this book—someone who has not given enough thought to retirement," says Marc, whose living expenses are covered by a modest pension from his former employer and a very modest salary from his teaching position.

Marc on the challenges of the profession

I think all that I dislike about teaching can be connected directly or indirectly to the amount of support given education by our society—that includes the community, local government, state government, and federal government. Problems largely center around time. It takes an inordinate amount of time to be well-prepared for class, to thoroughly evaluate the results of your assessment (homework, tests, papers, problem sets, lab write-ups, etc.), and to get to truly know the students in your classes. The amount of time you have is affected by the number of students in your classes, the number of classes per day, the number of preparations per day, and the amount of planning time during the day. These factors are determined by how much money the school district has. When these factors work against you (too many students per class, too many classes per day, too many preps per day), then the stress level becomes the dominant theme in your day.

Marc's advice for someone contemplating a career change:

If you are considering a career change to teaching because it seems like an easy alternative, I suggest that you reexamine your motivation. Teaching is hard work. I know of no other job that requires one to be on task continuously for the entire workday. No matter how expert you are in your field, being able to effectively pass that knowledge on to children is a very steep learning curve. Anyone who believes that teacher compensation is adequate is probably too naive to be a teacher. On the other hand, the intrinsic rewards are multiple. At the philosophical level, a teaching career is truly a way one can give back to society, give direction to our youth, and support the families of our communities. If you have a need to have a meaningful job, and you have the strength to look beyond the very real day-to-day challenges and stress of the classroom, then teaching can be a very rich and fulfilling career. At the personal level, the satisfaction of watching a struggling student succeed, an average student surpass his or her own and his or her parents' expectations, and an excellent student flourish to greatness is as thrilling as a roller coaster. I can also think of no better way to become an integral part of one's community. Not only are you participating in a critical societal role, you literally get to know the people in your community on a first-name basis. And if you are a public school teacher, you will have instant rapport with people at all levels in your community—from bankers and lawyers to car salesmen and grocery store clerks.

SARAH

College professor has no plans to retire

As the dean of education for a respected East Coast university, Sarah, 34, has no plans for retirement. "I hope to teach at the university until they throw me out," she joked.

If that day ever comes, Sarah can look forward to a financially secure retirement thanks to a strong 403(b) plan. Not only does she have quality vendor choices in her plan, but the university kicks in two dollars for every one dollar she contributes. Sarah, whose investment philosophy is "save as much as you can," currently directs 5% of her salary to a 403(b) account with TIAA-CREF.

While the retirement plan is nice, Sarah is motivated by her students. "More than anything else, it is the opportunity to hear the students' stories, and watch them make connections in their own classrooms," she says about the profession. "I think the professor gig is a great one. I am lucky to get to teach at the university full time, but still have the opportunity to get into schools and work with new teachers. It is great to help shape the next generation of teachers."

Sarah recently received an e-mail from a former student that summed up the intrinsic rewards of the profession. The email read: "Now I get it!"

HOMEWORK: Contact several colleagues who have recently retired. Query them about pension payout, savings, and medical benefits. Ask them for advice and pointers on planning for retirement.

CHAPTER FOUR

The Secret to Wealth Building: It's Elementary!

"Money is a terrible master but an excellent servant." — P.T. Barnum

Teachers love to make educational points with picture books. And no book explains wealth accumulation better than the picture book version of the classic money tale *The Richest Man in Babylon*. Adapted from the original story by George S. Clason, the colorful tale recounts how one man became the richest man in old Babylon. The story begins at a reunion of old school friends at the opulent palace of Arkad, the richest man in Babylon. Feelings of jealousy, curiosity, and anger are directed at Arkad and his seemingly lucky fate. Former classmates cannot comprehend how someone who was once their equal is now so wealthy.

"Arkad, you are more fortunate than we are," his friends declare.

"Why has Fickle Fate singled you out to enjoy all the good things of life?" they wonder.

"Surely you must have found favor with the Goddess of Good Luck," they speculate. Arkad only laughs at these declarations. In good time, he assures his guests, will the secret to wealth building be revealed.

After much dancing and celebration, Arkad finally begins to divulge the secret of his wealth. "It is not chance or fate," he explains, but rather that he has learned the laws that govern the building of wealth and has followed them in his daily life. His audience is duly impressed, and they press him for details. Arkad reminds his friends that he was not born into wealth, but that at a young age he realized that wealth was power. With wealth, he explained, one can delight the senses and gratify the soul. He then recounted laboring long and hard as a scribe in the Hall of Records. One day a man of great wealth came to Arkad needing to have some records copied. Arkad suggested that in exchange for his labor, perhaps the man would bestow upon him the secret to wealth. A deal was struck, and Arkad labored into the night. Upon completion of the task, the secret of wealth building was indeed revealed...

In a low, forceful tone, the wealthy man uttered these words: "A part of all you earn is yours to keep." So much for real estate, oil fields, and gold.

Arkad was angered. "Isn't all I earn mine to keep?" he inquired.

"Far from it," replied the man. "Do you not pay the sandal maker?" the man asked. "Do you not pay for the things that you eat?" the man continued. "You pay everyone but yourself!" the man explained.

"Pay yourself first," the man instructed. "Every gold piece you save is a slave to work for you. Every copper it earns is its child that also can earn for you. A part of all you earn is yours to keep. It should be no less than a tenth, no matter how little you earn."

So began Arkad's path to wealth accumulation. It was not without pitfalls, however. On one occasion, Arkad trusted the brickmaker to purchase jewels for him. A most foolish decision, it resulted in the loss of all his savings. On another occasion, Arkad treated himself to a great feast of food and spirits, for which his mentor laughed and scolded him, "You eat the children [the interest] of your savings. Then how do you expect them to work for you? First, get thee an army of golden slaves [saved money] and then many a rich banquet may you enjoy without regret."

Over time, Arkad learned to successfully employ the rules of wealth accumulation with spectacular results. While he trusted the brickmaker on matters of bricks, he trusted wise men schooled in the ways of finances with his money. Most importantly, however, Arkad always saved no less than ten percent of his earnings.

29

For most of us, accumulating wealth is not going to happen overnight. Nor should it—lest we blow it on great feasts of food and spirits. Little feasts with Budweiser and potato chips are probably okay. But by first paying ourselves no less than ten percent we can in time accumulate wealth—especially if we have a well-diversified portfolio of solid, quality investments (all of which will be covered in ensuing chapters). Fortunately, defined-benefit plans (pensions) and defined-contribution plans like the 403(b) and 457(b) by their very design make adhering to the principle of "pay yourself first" automatic. These plans require you to pay yourself first because contributions come directly out of your paycheck. This, too, will be explained in the chapters that follow.

The Five Laws of Gold from The Richest Man in Babylon

1. Gold comes gladly and in increasing quantities to any man (or woman) who will save not less than one-tenth of his earnings to create an estate for his future and that of his family.
2. Gold labors diligently and contentedly for the wise owner who finds profitable employment for it, multiplying even as the flocks of the field.
3. Gold clings to the protection of the cautious owner who invests it on the advice of men (and women) wise in its handling.
4. Gold slips away from the man (or woman) who invests it in businesses or for purposes with which he is not familiar or that are not approved by those skilled in its keep.
5. Gold flees from the man (or woman) who would force it to impossible earnings or who follows the alluring advice of tricksters and schemers or who trusts it to his own inexperience and romantic desires in investment.

NOTE: Unfortunately, the picture book version of *The Richest Man in Babylon*, which was published by Island Heritage, is currently out of print. The original 158-page chapter book by George S. Clason is readily available at bookstores.

HOMEWORK: Pick up a copy of *The Richest Man in Babylon* by George S. Clason. Urge three to four colleagues to do the same. Form a book club to read and discuss this timeless tale.

CHAPTER FIVE

Wealth-building Tools for Educators

....

"A billion here, a billion there, pretty soon it adds up to real money."
— Senator Everett Dirksen

Most educators have several powerful wealth-building tools
at their disposal—a defined-benefit plan (pension plan), a
defined-contribution plan (the 403(b) plan), and increasingly, a
second defined-contribution plan, the 457(b). Most teachers are
also eligible to contribute to a Roth IRA. Each of these plans is
described here.

DEFINED-BENEFIT PLANS (PENSION PLANS)

The first wealth-building tool available to most educators is the
defined-benefit plan (also called a DB plan), or pension plan.
Upon retirement, these plans promise an income for life, based
on years of service and a retirement factor determined by each
state. The plan's benefit is defined by a formula specific to your
employer, but it generally resembles the following: a percentage
(often around 2 percent, but sometimes lower) multiplied by the
number of years worked multiplied by the average of your three
highest-paid years. EXAMPLE: Thirty years worked multiplied by
2 percent entitles a teacher to 60 percent of the average of his
or her three-highest paid years. Other factors that may be taken
into consideration include unused sick leave and a longevity factor
for working more than thirty years and/or working beyond sixty

years of age. Most plans allow a retiree to add a survivor's benefit provision, guaranteeing that a loved one would continue receiving a payout when the retiree passes away. Adding such a benefit would modify or reduce the payout. For specific payout rules applicable to your situation, contact the state agency operating your plan. Many plans now have sophisticated Internet-based information including calculators that allow employees to project payouts.

CALIFORNIA TEACHERS' PENSION DATA

Retirement date	June 30, 2003	June 30, 1994
Number of retirements	11,189	7,152
Average service credit	27.9 years	27 years
Average unmodified monthly benefit	$3,676	$2,187
Average age at retirement	61.2	60.9

SOURCE: California State Teachers' Retirement System, accessible online at *www.calstrs.com*.

Contribution to a pension plan is automatic, it is usually mandatory, and it lowers your taxes. This means that you must contribute each pay period and that these contributions lower your taxable income—all very good things. You usually do not have a choice to opt out. While forced labor is a bad thing, forced savings should be viewed as a good thing for one obvious reason: it obligates you to save. For some individuals this is the only way they are able to accumulate savings. Plus, for every dollar you contribute to a pension plan, your taxable income is reduced by one dollar. Let's say that you are a single teacher earning $50,000 a year and contributing $200 per month to a DB plan—for a total yearly contribution of $2,400 (12 pay periods times $200). Instead of being taxed on income of $50,000, you are taxed on income of $47,600 ($50,000 less the $2,400 pension plan contribution). In this scenario you have lowered your taxes by $600 (assuming that you are in the 25% marginal tax bracket), and you have still contributed $2,400 to your DB plan. It does not take a math teacher to know that this is a very good thing.

In a pension plan (also called a DB plan) the employer (typically the state) makes all investment decisions, as opposed to in a defined-contribution plan (also called a DC plan) such as a 403(b) or a 457(b), where the individual (or an advisor) makes all investment decisions. (DC plans will be covered later in this chapter.)

A pension plan works much like Social Security. In fact, in many states teachers contribute to a DB plan in lieu of Social Security. In some states teachers contribute to both a pension plan and Social Security. Each state has its own pension plan or plans in which teachers participate. All plans essentially work the same. Each pay period you make a mandatory contribution of a percentage of salary (roughly 6 percent to 8 percent). Your employer also makes a contribution that is based on an actuarial formula, ensuring that sufficient funds will be in the plan to guarantee your monthly income benefit at retirement. Employer contributions do not further lower your taxes. Upon retiring, you receive a specific amount each month based on the factors explained earlier, including salary history, years, and so forth.

PENSION PLAN FAQs

What are your options if you leave the profession early?

You have three options if you leave teaching early.

1. *Leave your contributions in the plan*

   Most plans allow you to leave your contributions in the plan and draw a payout when you reach eligibility. Contact your pension administrator to determine your projected payout. If your payout will be a small one, it may make more sense to go with Option 2.

2. *Move the balance*

   Most plans allow you to move your balance into a rollover IRA. This will avoid withdrawal penalties and delay taxes until withdrawal. Plus, you will be free to direct your investments to the financial institution of your choice. Under this scenario you may not touch the money. Instead, all exchanges of money must be handled by the state agency holding the money and the financial institution receiving the money. This is known as a direct rollover or a trustee-to-trustee transfer. Your pension administrator and the financial institution to which you wish to transfer your balance will be able to provide detailed directions.

3. *Withdraw the money*

   You can also withdraw the money upon termination of employment, but you will be hit with withdrawal penalties and taxes. Withdrawals will be taxed as ordinary income and may be subject to a 10 percent penalty imposed by the IRS. This option runs directly counter to the philosophy of this book.

NOTE: When you pull your money out of your pension plan prior to retirement (as described in options 2 and 3), you do not receive money that was contributed by your employer.

What are your options if you leave to teach under a different pension system?

Rules vary by plan and by state, so the best sources of information for your particular situation will be your former pension provider and your new pension provider. Contact both of these entities to get specific details. In many cases you will be able to purchase service credit (years worked) in your new system with pension money from your old system. Some states have more than one pension plan and will grant reciprocity for teachers moving between different systems.

Can you purchase pension service credit using 403(b) and 457(b) money?

Yes. Thanks to the Economic Growth and Tax Relief Reconciliation Act (EGTRRA) of 2001, employees of state and local governments are able to transfer assets from their 403(b) and 457(b) accounts to state defined benefit plans in order to purchase some types of past service credits. Contact your pension administrator for specific rules about service credit purchases.

Most DB plans have extensive education resources available, including Internet-based help, toll-free telephone help lines, and retirement planning workshops. It is recommended that you become familiar with the workings of your specific plan as soon as possible. Do not wait until you are just a few years from retirement to get wise to this information.

As *Teach and Retire Rich* was going to print, major changes to traditional pensions were being debated. In Washington, DC, President Bush was seeking historic changes to Social Security, while in California a proposal to greatly alter the pension systems that serve teachers and others was being pushed. The outcome of these proposals cannot be predicted, but what is certain is that the responsibility for retirement will continue to shift from government and employer to worker. Dubbed the "ownership society," this movement demands that employees take an active role in planning and funding their retirement. Fear not—the concepts presented in this book will help all employees survive and thrive in such an environment. Knowledge is power, and as President Franklin Delano Roosevelt said, "the only thing to fear is fear itself." So fear not, but save a lot.

HOMEWORK: Contact the agency that manages your pension plan. This information is most readily available via the Internet. If not, contact your human resources department. Find out the pension payout formula and other operational information. Estimate your pension payout based on how long you plan to teach. The websites of many plans include calculators to aid you in this process. Share what you learn with at least two of your colleagues.

THE 403(b) DEFINED-CONTRIBUTION PLANS

The 403(b) is a tax-deferred retirement savings plan for employees of educational institutions and certain nonprofit organizations. The name refers to the section of the Internal Revenue Code that governs the plan. The 403(b) was created in 1958 and is sometimes referred to as a tax-deferred annuity (TDA). Similar to a 401(k) plan, which covers private-sector workers, the plan is also known as defined-contribution plan (or DC plan). Upon retirement, 403(b) savings can be used to supplement a pension plan or can serve as a main retirement plan for those not covered by a pension plan.

Like contributions to a pension plan, contributions to a 403(b) are set up to occur regularly. However, contributions to a 403(b) are not mandatory and enrollment is not automatic. You do not have to participate in a 403(b). In fact, many teachers do not participate: the latest figures from the Spectrem Group, a financial consulting firm, reveal that only two in five teachers take advantage of this savings vehicle. The 403(b) plan, like the Roth IRA and the 457(b) plan, requires discipline and education. To participate, you must opt in, and you have to manage the investments or have an agent or advisor manage the investments for you. With a 403(b) you are free to invest in annuities, variable annuities, and mutual funds, but not in individual stocks. (What to invest in, where to invest, and how to allocate investments are discussed in Chapters Six through Eleven.)

As in a pension plan, a key benefit of the 403(b) is that contributions reduce taxable income. Again, each dollar contributed to a 403(b) lowers taxable income by one dollar.

In the earlier example, it was hypothesized that a teacher earning $50,000 contributes $2,400 annually to a pension plan ($200 per month). Instead of being taxed on an income of $50,000, this teacher would be taxed on $47,600, which saved him or her $600 in taxes. Now imagine if this teacher contributed an additional $100 a month to a 403(b). This $1,200 403(b) contribution would further reduce the taxable income to $46,400, and save an additional $300 in taxes (again assuming that the teacher is in the 25 percent marginal tax bracket). Thanks to mandatory contributions to a pension plan and voluntary contributions to a 403(b) plan, $900 has been saved in taxes. In effect this money saved on taxes ($900) can partially fund the $1,200 investment in the 403(b). Furthermore, all earnings in a 403(b) grow tax-deferred until the time of retirement, when withdrawals are taxed as ordinary income. This triple benefit (reduction in taxes, tax-free growth, and establishment of long-term savings accounts) is a core principle of the *Teach and Retire Rich* philosophy.

TAX SAVINGS FROM PENSION AND 403(b) CONTRIBUTIONS

This chart assumes a single teacher in the 25% marginal tax bracket.

	with pension and 403(b)	*without pension and 403(b)*
Salary	$50,000	$50,000
Pension contributions	$2,400	—
403(b) contributions	$1,200	—
Taxable income	$46,400	$50,000
TAXES SAVED	*$900*	

403(b) FAQs

How do you start a 403(b)?

There are four steps.

1. Ask your employer for a list of investment companies that are available to manage your savings. This is typically known as the vendor list.

2. Research several investment companies from this list. (What to invest in, where to invest, and how to allocate investments are discussed in Chapters Six through Eleven.) Set up a 403(b) account with your chosen investment company or companies.

3. Determine the amount of money you wish to contribute monthly. Most companies require at least $50 per month. You will also be asked to name a beneficiary who will receive your investment in the event of your death. Your vendor will be able to provide details on naming a beneficiary.

4. Finally, complete a salary-reduction agreement for your employer. This is an arrangement under which you (the employee) agree to take a reduction in salary. Do not panic! The amount reduced is directed to the 403(b) investment(s) you select. Contributions are known as elective deferrals and are excluded from your income as described earlier.

Agent/advisor services

You are free to set up and manage your own 403(b) plan. Many plans provide the option to invest through a vendor representative or agent. You are also free to work with an independent financial advisor. For more details on selecting and using an agent or advisor, see the Seventh Commandment in Chapter Eleven.

How much can you contribute to a 403(b)?

Year	Contribution limit [1]	Age 50 catch-up [2]
2004	$13,000	$3,000
2005	$14,000	$4,000
2006	$15,000	$5,000

Contribution limits will be indexed for inflation after 2006.

[1] You can contribute up to 100 percent of your total includable compensation as long as it is less than or equal to the contribution limit. [2] These amounts are for participants who are age 50 or older and are in addition to the regular contribution limit.

Additionally, there is a provision of the Internal Revenue Code that temporarily increases the elective deferral limit (maximum contribution amount) for eligible employees. This increase is known as the fifteen year rule. This provision increases the maximum contribution amount by as much as $3,000 per year (see the preceding table). To qualify you must have completed at least fifteen years of service with the same employer (the years of service need not be consecutive), and you cannot have contributed more than an average of $5,000 to a 403(b) in previous years. The increase in your elective-deferral limit (maximum contribution amount) cannot exceed $3,000 per year under this provision, up to a $15,000 lifetime maximum. If you believe you are eligible for the fifteen-year-rule, you should consult with a tax or financial planning professional concerning the limits on your contributions.

What are your options when changing jobs?

You have four options.

1. *Move the balance into a new plan—403(b), 401(k), or 457(b)*

   You may move the money into your new employer's 403(b) plan. You may also roll a 403(b) into a 401(k) or governmental 457(b), and vice versa. Not all plans allow such transfers, so be sure that you check with your new employer and your vendors (current and future) for the exact rules covering your situation.

2. *Move the balance into a rollover IRA*

   You are also permitted to move 403(b) money into a rollover IRA with a financial institution of your choice. A rollover can be handled two ways. If you initiate a direct rollover all exchange of money is handled by the institution currently holding your 403(b) and the financial institution that will receive the money. Direct rollovers, known as trustee-to-trustee transfers, will delay taxes until you begin making withdrawals (assumed to be at retirement). If you choose to manage the rollover yourself and take possession of the funds, the money will be subject to a mandatory 20 percent federal withholding. For more details, contact both the company you currently invest with and the company you will be rolling over to.

3. *Leave the balance where it is*

   You may leave the money where it is, especially if you like your investment choices. The money will continue to grow tax-deferred.

4. *Withdraw the money*

   You may withdraw the money upon termination of employment, but you will be subject to the mandatory 20 percent federal withholding on amounts withdrawn that are eligible to be rolled over, an early-withdrawal penalty, and taxes. For more details check with your vendor. Withdrawing money prior to retirement runs directly counter to the philosophy of this book.

NOTE: Before transferring, rolling over, or withdrawing money, check to see if your vendor imposes surrender charges.

Can a loan be taken from a 403(b)?

In order to allow temporary access to your 403(b) account, the Internal Revenue Service (IRS) permits loans. There are, however, some limits on the amount. Generally, the loan cannot exceed the smaller of:

- $50,000, or
- one-half of your account balance (though if your account balance is less than $20,000 you may borrow up to $10,000 if you have that much in your account).

In applying these limits, all of your 403(b) accounts must be combined and aggregated with any loans from other retirement plans you might have, such as a 401(k).

Loans must be repaid by making repayments of principal and interest at least quarterly. Unless the loan is made to acquire your principal residence, it must be repaid within five years.

Failure to make scheduled loan repayments will cause the outstanding loan balance to be included in your gross income and subject to the federal 10% early distribution penalty. Additionally, such a loan default may impair your ability to make loans against your 403(b) account in the future.

Loans are required to charge interest. The lender keeps those amounts that you pay in interest, so interest payments will not be a part of your retirement savings. Plus, when you borrow from your 403(b) you are, in effect, borrowing from your future. Borrowing from your 403(b) runs counter to the philosophy of this book. Steer clear of any company or representative that touts the loan provisions of their 403(b) products. Therefore, loans should be used only when absolutely necessary.

43

Not all vendors allow loans from 403(b) accounts. Contact your vendor for complete details regarding loan availability, interest rates, repayment options, etc.

Can hardship withdrawals be made from a 403(b)?

Yes. 403(b) plans allow for withdrawal of funds if a participant is under severe financial distress and has no other resources available. A hardship withdrawal may be made for the following:

- unreimbursed medical expenses for the participant or his or her spouse and dependents
- a down payment on a primary residence
- tuition and fees for higher education needs, but only for twelve months
- to prevent eviction or foreclosure on a primary residence

Hardship withdrawals are not exempt from the 10 percent early withdrawal penalty imposed by the IRS. Furthermore, withdrawals are subject to taxation as ordinary income in the year withdrawn.

To qualify, you must certify that you have no other recourse, including the possibility of taking a loan. You are also prohibited from contributing to a 403(b) for the six months following your withdrawal. The IRS makes it tough to access money this way for a reason: they do not want you to use the 403(b) as a form of short-term savings.

Also, while the IRS permits withdrawals, it is allowable for a plan sponsor (the employer) to prohibit them. The employer has some responsibility in making hardship withdrawals. The employer must approve the hardship, basing its decision on written information provided by the employee about the hardship. The employer must determine, based on the facts, whether or not the employee has an "immediate and heavy financial need." For exact details on your situation, you should contact both your vendor and a tax professional before proceeding.

What happens to a 403(b) if you become disabled?

Withdrawal of 403(b) money is permitted in cases of disability, as defined by the IRS. Consult the IRS, your vendor or a tax professional for more details.

What happens to a 403(b) in the event of a divorce?

Some or all of the balance in a 403(b) account may be transferred to a spouse as part of a divorce settlement. Distribution to an "alternate payee" will be permitted if pursuant to a qualified domestic relations order (QDRO). This is a decree, judgment, or order that meets the following qualification requirements of the Internal Revenue Code:

- The order must have been issued under a state's community property or other domestic relations law.
- It must relate to the provision of alimony, child support or the property rights of a spouse, former spouse, child or other dependent (alternate payee).
- It must assign to the alternate payee the right to receive all or a portion of the participant's plan benefits.
- It must clearly specify (1) the names and addresses of each alternate payee, (2) the amount or percentage of the participant's benefit to be paid to each alternate payee, (3) the period of time over which the order applies, and (4) each plan to which the order applies.

If a distribution is made to a spouse or former spouse under a QDRO, the distribution may be rolled into a qualified plan or IRA that the spouse or former spouse has. Distribution to any other alternate payee is not eligible for rollover. It is highly recommended that you seek the counsel of a qualified attorney in the event of divorce. It may also be necessary to speak with a tax or financial planning professional. For more information on divorce, see Chapter Twelve.

What happens to a 403(b) in the event of a death?

Assets in the 403(b) will be passed first to the individual (or individuals) named as beneficiary.

What happens to a 403(b) at retirement?

You have four options.

1. *Withdraw the money*

   You are free to begin withdrawals free of IRS penalty
   upon retirement (assumed to be at least age fifty-five).
   Withdrawals will be taxed as ordinary income.

2. *Take SEPP withdrawals*

   If you retired in a calendar year before the one in which you
   reached age 55, you may withdraw 403(b) money through a
   series of Substantially Equal Periodic Payments (SEPP). Once
   you begin the SEPP payments, they must continue for five
   years or until you reach age 59-1/2, whichever comes later.
   Withdrawals will be taxed as ordinary income.

3. *Leave the money where it is*

   You may leave the money where it is, especially if you like
   your investment choices. The money will continue to grow
   tax-deferred.

4. *Move the balance into a rollover IRA*

   You are also permitted to move 403(b) money into a rollover
   IRA with a financial institution of your choice. This will delay
   taxes until you begin making withdrawals. A rollover can be
   handled two ways. If you initiate a direct rollover all exchange
   of money is handled by the institution currently holding
   your 403(b) and the financial institution that will receive the
   money. This is known as a trustee-to-trustee transfer. If you
   choose to initiate the rollover yourself and take possession
   of the funds, the money will be subject to a mandatory 20

percent federal withholding. For more details, contact both the company you currently invest with and the company you will be rolling over to.

NOTE: Before transferring, rolling over, or withdrawing money, check to see if your vendor imposes surrender charges. Also, if you are still working, you may begin to make penalty-free withdrawals during the calendar year in which you reach age 59-1/2. Generally, you must begin to take withdrawals from your 403(b) no later than April 1 of the year following the year in which you turn age 70-1/2. If you are still working, you can delay withdrawal from your 403(b) until April 1 following the year in which you retire.

47

THE 90-24 TRANSFER

The 403(b) contains a special provision (90-24) that allows individuals to transfer 403(b) money to a vendor of their choice—even one that is not available through their employer. The caveat is that your employer's plan and your existing vendor must permit transfers. The IRS allows transfers, but it does not require that they be made. A 90-24 transfer is a trustee-to-trustee transfer. To avoid a penalty, you must never take possession of the funds. Instead, all exchange of money must be handled by the trustees holding and receiving the money. Many 403(b) investments—particularly insurance-based annuity and variable annuity products—charge stiff exit penalties that often last up to seven years. Be aware of all surrender charges before initiating a transfer. If penalties exist, one course of action is to transfer only money that has been invested past the penalty phase. As new money passes the penalty threshold, transfer it. The financial institution you wish to transfer into should be able to answer any of your questions. NOTE: Proposed IRS regulations set to take effect in 2006 would eliminate the ability to transfer to an outside-of-plan vendor. Visit *www.irs.gov* and *www.403bwise.com* for the latest information on the proposed changes.

Other 403(b) items of note

- As an individual, you cannot set up your own 403(b) plan. It must be offered through an employer.

- Universal availability rules require that all employees who work twenty or more hours a week be allowed to participate. This often includes substitute teachers. Employers must take special care to comply with this provision. Noncompliance could result in the entire plan losing its tax-favored treatment. Employers do not have to restrict participation to those who work twenty hours a week. They may make the plan available to all employees.

- When the 403(b) was created in 1958, participants could invest only in insurance products. In 1974, Congress added paragraph 7 to the 403(b), allowing participants to invest in mutual funds through a 403(b)(7) custodial account. For the purposes of this book, the term 403(b) refers to both 403(b) and 403(b)(7) accounts.

- Participation in a 403(b) will not reduce your Social Security benefits. Salary contributions to a 403(b) reduce taxable compensation for federal (and in most instances, state) income tax purposes only. Contributions do not reduce wages for the purpose of determining FICA taxes or determining Social Security benefits.

- A special Saver's Tax Credit is available for low-income savers. Eligible savers will receive a tax credit of up to 50 percent on up to $2,000 in contributions to an IRA, 403(b), 457(b), SIMPLE, or 401(k) plan. Joint filers whose adjusted gross income (AGI) is less than $30,000 are eligible for the full 50 percent credit; joint filers with AGI between $30,000 and $32,500 are eligible for a 20 percent credit; and joint filers with an AGI between $32,500 and $50,000 are eligible for a 10 percent credit. Eligibility for single filers is one-half the threshold for joint filers. EXAMPLE: A single earner with an AGI less than $15,000 would be eligible for the full 50 percent tax credit. This provision is set to expire in 2006.

- If you have both a 403(b) and 457(b) available to you but cannot fully fund each plan, first fund the plan in which you are given an employer match. If no match exists, fund the plan with the best investment choices first.

- There has been some discussion recently in government circles about merging most employer-sponsored retirement plans, including the 403(b), the 457(b), and the 401(k), into one plan with one set of rules. For the latest information on any proposed rule changes to the 403(b), be a regular visitor to the 403(b)wise website at *www.403bwise.com*.

49

- At the end of 2004 the IRS proposed new regulations for the 403(b). If approved, these changes would take effect in 2006. Visit *www.irs.gov* and *www.403bwise.com* for the latest information on the proposed changes.

- A great place to get 403(b) questions answered is on the 403(b) Discussion Board, which can be accessed from the home page of *www.403bwise.com*.

Further details on the 403(b) can be found in IRS Publication 571, *Tax-Sheltered Annuity Plans (403(b) Plans) for Employees of Public Schools and Certain Tax-Exempt Organizations*. This publication may be downloaded from the IRS website at *www.irs.gov*. It may also be obtained by calling 1-800-TAX-FORMS.

HOMEWORK

PART 1: Obtain a 403(b) vendor list from your employer. Keep it handy as you progress through this book.

PART 2: Display the following prominently in the staff lounge: "To 403(b) or not to 403(b), that is the question. To 403(b) is the answer." Sign your name. This should lead to a host of questions (some, perhaps, about your sanity). Your job is to provide the answers.

THE GOVERNMENTAL 457(B) (SOMETIMES REFERRED TO AS A DEFERRED-COMPENSATION PLAN)

NOTE: There are several variations of 457 plans. This book will focus on the governmental 457(b), which covers most teachers.

The 457(b) is another tax-deferred retirement savings plan for employees of state and local governmental agencies, which includes public school employees. The name refers to the section of the Internal Revenue Code that governs the plan. The 457(b) was created in 1978 and is sometimes referred to as a deferred-compensation plan. Thanks to the Economic Growth and Tax-Relief Reconciliation Act of 2001 (EGTRRA), teachers are eligible to contribute the maximum elective-deferral limit to both a 403(b) and a 457(b). This means that participants with enough includable compensation can now contribute $14,000 (for 2005) to each plan—for a whopping $28,000. Catch-up rules increase contribution amounts even further. Obviously it is the rare teacher who is able to save this amount of money, but it is nice to know this option is available for those who can. Speaking of availability, while nearly all teachers have access to a 403(b), not all have access to a 457(b). The good news is that an increasing number of employers are now making the 457(b) available as well. If your employer does not yet offer a 457(b) plan, lobby them to do so. Point out the advantages and the ability to further reduce taxable income. Like in the 403(b), contributions are not mandatory. So again, this plan requires discipline.

Traditionally, the 457(b) covered state and local government employees, which often included teachers. In the past, teachers who wished to contribute to both a 403(b) and a 457(b) were limited to the total aggregate amount of the 457(b) (only $8,500 at the time). The Economic Growth and Tax-Relief Reconciliation Act of 2001 (EGTRRA) repealed this coordination of contributions between 457(b) plans and 403(b) plans allowing participants with enough includable compensation to contribute the maximum elective-deferral limit to each plan. For 2005, this is $14,000 to each plan for a total contribution of $28,000. Catch-up rules increase contribution amounts even further.

457(B) FAQS
How do you start a 457(b)?

There are five steps.

1. Ask your employer for a list of the participating investment companies available to you. This is typically known as the vendor list.
2. Ask to see the plan document. Unlike the 403(b), employers must have a plan document that specifies the exact rules of the 457(b). This will be your best source of information for your particular plan.
3. Research several investment companies from this list (What to invest in, where to invest, and how to allocate investments are discussed in Chapters Six through Eleven.) Set up a 457(b) account with your chosen investment company or companies.
4. Determine the amount of money you wish to contribute monthly. Most companies require at least $50 per month. You will also be asked to name a beneficiary who will receive your investment in the event of your death. Your vendor will be able to provide details on naming a beneficiary.

5. Finally, complete a salary-reduction agreement for your employer. This is an arrangement under which you (the employee) agree to take a reduction in salary. Do not panic! The amount reduced is directed to the 457(b) investment(s) you select. Contributions are known as "elective deferrals" and are excluded from your income as described earlier.

Agent/advisor services

You are free to set up and manage your own 457(b) plan. Many 457(b) plans give you the option of investing through a vendor representative or agent. You are also free to work with an independent financial advisor. For more details on using an agent or advisor, see the Seventh Commandment in Chapter Eleven.

How much can you contribute to a 457(b)?

Year	Contribution limit[1]	Age 50 catch-up[2]
2004	$13,000	$3,000
2005	$14,000	$4,000
2006	$15,000	$5,000

Contribution limits will be indexed for inflation after 2006.

[1] You can contribute up to 100 percent of your total includable compensation as long as it is less than or equal to the contribution limit. [2] These amounts are for participants who are age 50 or older and are in addition to the regular contribution limit.

Additionally, there is a provision known as the three-year-rule, which temporarily doubles the contribution limit when a participant is three years from normal retirement age, as defined by the plan document. Consult your plan document for exact rules on the three-year-rule specific to your plan.

What are your options when changing jobs?

You have four options.

1. *Move the balance into a new plan—457(b), 401(k), or 403(b)*
   You may move the money into your new employer's governmental 457(b) plan. You may also roll a 457(b) into a 401(k) or a 403(b), and vice versa. Not all plans allow such transfers, so be sure that you check with your new employer and your vendors (current and future) for the exact rules covering your situation.

2. *Move the balance into a rollover IRA*
   You are also permitted to move 457(b) money into a rollover IRA with a financial institution of your choice. A rollover can be handled two ways. If you initiate a direct rollover all exchange of money is handled by the institution currently holding your 457(b) and the financial institution that will receive the money. Direct rollovers, known as trustee-to-trustee transfers, will delay taxes until you begin making withdrawals (assumed to be at retirement). If you choose to manage the rollover yourself and take possession of the funds, the money will be subject to a mandatory 20 percent federal withholding. For more details, contact both the company you currently invest with and the company you will be rolling over to.

3. *Leave the balance where it is*

    You may leave the money where it is, especially if you like your investment choices. The money will continue to grow tax-deferred.

4. *Withdraw the money*

    A big advantage to the 457(b) plan is that it is not subject to the age 59-1/2 withdrawal rule. This means that there is no 10 percent penalty for early withdrawal upon termination of employment. If you roll your 457(b) money into a rollover IRA (as described earlier), you will lose this valuable benefit. If you take money out, it may be subject to the mandatory 20 percent federal withholding if the distribution is an eligible rollover distribution. Check with your vendor for exact rules. Withdrawals from your 457(b) will still be taxed as ordinary income. Withdrawing money prior to retirement runs directly counter to the philosophy of this book.

NOTE: Before transferring, rolling over, or withdrawing money, check to see if your vendor imposes surrender charges.

Can a loan be taken from a 457(b)?

Many 457(b) plans and vendors (though not all) allow loans. Your plan document will spell out specific rules regarding loans. Think very seriously before initiating a loan from your 457(b) because you are, in effect, borrowing from your future. Borrowing from your 457(b) runs counter to the philosophy of this book. Steer clear of any company or representative that touts the loan provisions of their 457(b) products.

Can hardship withdrawals be made from a 457(b)?

457(b) plans may, but are not required to, permit distributions to participants or beneficiaries who are faced with unforeseeable emergencies. The plan must define "unforeseeable emergency" as a severe financial hardship resulting from any of the following:

- an illness or accident of the individual, the individual's spouse, or the individual's dependent
- loss of the individual's property due to a casualty
- similar extraordinary and unforeseeable circumstances arising as a result of events beyond the control of the individual

Examples of unforeseeable emergencies might include:

- imminent foreclosure of, or eviction from, the individual's primary residence
- the need to pay for medical expenses or prescription medicines
- funeral expenses for a spouse or dependent

Please note that home purchases and tuition payments are not considered unforeseeable emergencies.

Whether an individual is faced with an eligible unforeseeable emergency is determined based on the relevant facts and circumstances of each case. Even if an unforeseeable emergency exists, the distribution cannot be made if the emergency can be relieved in any of the following ways:

- through reimbursement or compensation from insurance or otherwise
- by liquidation of the individual's assets, to the extent that

such liquidation would not in itself cause a severe financial hardship

- by cessation of deferrals to the plan

Your employer must approve any distribution. If granted, the emergency distribution cannot exceed the amount deemed reasonably necessary to satisfy the emergency need, including any amount anticipated to pay any federal, state, or local income taxes or penalties as a result of the distribution.

What happens to a 457(b) if you become disabled?

Unlike the 403(b), disability itself is not a distributable event. However, it may be considered an unforseeable emergency and you may be able to withdraw money, subject to certain rules and restrictions. Consult your employer for exact rules.

What happens to a 457(b) in the event of a divorce?

Some or all of the balance in your 457(b) account may be transferred to a spouse as part of a divorce settlement. Distribution to an alternate payee will be permitted if it is made pursuant to a qualified domestic relations order (QDRO). This is a decree, judgment, or order that meets the following qualification requirements of the Internal Revenue Code:

- The order must have been issued under a state's community-property or other domestic relations law.
- It must relate to the provision of alimony, child support, or the property rights of a spouse, former spouse, child, or other dependent (alternate payee).

- It must assign to the alternate payee the right to receive all or a portion of the participant's plan benefits.
- It must clearly specify (1) the names and addresses of each alternate payee, (2) the amount or percentage of the participant's benefit to be paid to each alternate payee, (3) the period of time over which the order applies, and (4) each plan to which the order applies.

If a distribution is made to a spouse or former spouse under a QDRO, the distribution may be rolled into a qualified plan or IRA that the spouse or former spouse has. Distribution to any other alternate payee is not eligible for rollover. It is highly recommended that individuals seek the counsel of a qualified attorney in the event of divorce. It may also be necessary to speak with a tax or financial professional. For more information on divorce, see Chapter Twelve.

What happens to a 457(b) in the event of a death?

Assets in the 457(b) will be passed first to the individual (or individuals) named as beneficiary.

What happens to a 457(b) at retirement?

You have three options.

1. *Withdraw the money*

   You are free to begin withdrawals free of IRS penalty upon retirement. Withdrawals cannot begin until separation of service, and they will be taxed as ordinary income.

2. *Leave the money where it is*

   You may leave the money where it is, especially if you like

your investment choices. The money will continue to grow tax-deferred.

3. *Move the balance into a rollover IRA*

   You are also permitted to move 457(b) money into a rollover IRA with a financial institution of your choice. This will delay taxes until you begin making withdrawals. A rollover can be handled two ways. If you initiate a direct rollover all exchange of money is handled by the institution currently holding your 457(b) and the financial institution that will receive the money. This is known as a trustee-to-trustee transfer. If you choose to initiate the rollover yourself and take possession of the funds, the money will be subject to a mandatory 20 percent federal withholding. For more details, contact both the company you currently invest with and the company you will be rolling over to. Before you initiate a transfer, check to see if surrender penalties apply.

NOTE: Before transferring, rolling over, or withdrawing money, check to see if your vendor imposes surrender charges. Also, if you are still working, you may begin to make penalty-free withdrawals during the calendar year in which you reach age 70-1/2. Generally, you must begin to take withdrawals from your 457(b) no later than April 1 of the year following the year in which you turn age 70-1/2. If you are still working, you can delay withdrawal from your 457(b) until April 1 following the year in which you retire.

Other 457(b) items of note

- Your employer must create a plan document detailing the specific rules of the plan. As mentioned earlier, your plan document will be your best source of information about your plan.

- As an individual, you cannot set up your own 457(b) plan. It must be offered through an employer.

- 457(b) plans are subject to protection from creditors thanks to the Small Business Job Protection Act of 1996. This provision came about after Orange County, California, declared bankruptcy in the mid-1990s.

- Unlike the 403(b) plan, there is no universal accessibility with the 457(b). This means that employers are not required to make the plan available to all employees. However, any individual who performs service for the employer, including independent contractors, is eligible to participate in the plan if permitted by the employer.

- Participation in a 457(b) will not reduce your Social Security benefits. Salary contributions to a 457(b) reduce taxable compensation for federal (and in most instances, state) income tax purposes only. Contributions do not reduce wages for the purpose of determining FICA taxes or determining Social Security benefits.

- A special Saver's Tax Credit is available for low-income savers. Eligible savers will receive a tax credit of up to 50 percent on up to $2,000 in contributions to an IRA, 403(b), 457(b), SIMPLE, or 401(k) plan. Joint filers whose adjusted gross income (AGI) is less than $30,000 are eligible for the full 50 percent credit; joint filers with AGI between $30,000 and $32,500 are eligible for a 20 percent credit; and joint filers with an AGI between $32,500 and $50,000 are eligible for a 10 percent credit. Eligibility for single filers is one-half the threshold for joint filers. EXAMPLE: A single earner with an AGI less than $15,000 would be eligible for the full 50 percent tax credit. This provision is set to expire in 2006.

- Withdrawals cannot begin until separation of service. This means that you cannot have access to 457(b) money at age 59-1/2 if you are still working.

- If you have both a 457(b) and 403(b) available at work but cannot fully fund each plan, first fund the plan in which you are given an employer match. If no match exists, fund the plan with the best investment choices first.

- There has been some discussion recently in government circles about merging most employee sponsored retirement plans, including the 457(b), the 403(b), and the 401(k), into one plan with one set of rules. For the latest information on any proposed rule changes, visit the 457(b)wise website at *www.457bwise.com.*

- A great place to get 457(b) questions answered is on the 457(b) Discussion Board, which may be accessed from the home page of *www.457bwise.com.*

HOMEWORK

PART 1: Check with your employer to see if a 457(b) is offered. If it is, obtain a copy of both the vendor list and the plan document. Set both of these aside for reference as you progress through this book.

PART 2: Display the following prominently in the staff lounge: "Can the numbers 4-5-7 equate to retirement heaven? They can." Sign your name. As with the previously suggested 403(b) assignment, this should lead to a host of questions (and probably to even more questions about your sanity). Your job again is to provide the answers.

THE ROTH IRA

With meager contribution limits ($4,000 for years 2005 through 2007) and no ability to reduce taxable income, you might ask what is there to love about the Roth IRA? Like the seed that becomes the beautiful flower, the payoff for the Roth is down the road. The investor who reaches age 59-1/2 and has held a Roth IRA for at least five years can enjoy tax-free withdrawal of their savings. This last point—tax-free withdrawals—cannot be underscored enough given that withdrawal from pension plans and from 403(b) and 457(b) plans are taxed as ordinary income. The bet with the Roth IRA is that the ability to make tax-free withdrawals in the future will be greater than the upfront tax break realized through these employer-sponsored plans.

How much can you contribute to a Roth IRA?

Year	Contribution limit	Age 50 catch-up[1]
2005	$4,000	$ 500
2006	$4,000	$1,000
2007	$4,000	$1,000
2008	$5,000	$1,000

[1] These amounts are for participants who are age 50 or older and are in addition to the regular contribution limit.

Another advantage of a Roth IRA is that you are free to invest in any financial institution you choose. This can be a big deal for those stuck with poor 403(b) or 457(b) investment choices at work.

Who is eligible to contribute to a Roth IRA?

- Single workers earning up to $95,000 (adjusted gross income). Eligibility phases out at $110,000 (AGI).
- Married couples (filing jointly) earning up to $150,000 (adjusted gross income). Eligibility phases out at $160,000 (AGI).

See a tax professional for exact eligibility rules relevant to your situation.

How do you start a Roth IRA?

Simply contact a vendor of your choice. (What to invest in, where to invest, and how to allocate investments are discussed in Chapters Six through Eleven.) Unlike a pension plan or 403(b) and 457(b) contributions, Roth IRA contributions do not come directly out of a paycheck. Instead, the individual must arrange contributions. You can make things simple by setting up an automatic contribution plan that regularly transfers money from a checking or brokerage account into your Roth IRA. Your investment company should be only too happy to arrange this.

Other Roth IRA items of note

- Tax-free withdrawals from a Roth IRA prior to age 59-1/2 may be made in case of disability, first-time home purchase, or death.

- Withdrawal of Roth IRA contributions (not earnings) may be made tax-free at any time. EXAMPLE: You contribute $2,000 to a Roth IRA and over time the value grows to $2,500. You are eligible to withdraw the $2,000 in contributions, but not the $500 in earnings.

- The Roth IRA was named for its creator, the late Senator William Roth, Jr. of Delaware.

- Since the Roth IRA is not an employer-sponsored plan, no action needs to be taken when you change employers.

- As long as you do not exceed the income provisions (as described earlier), you can contribute to a Roth IRA and both a 403(b) and a 457(b).

- If you are stuck with poor investment choices in your 403(b) or 457(b), it may make more sense to contribute to a Roth IRA instead.

- With a Roth IRA, you have the ability to invest directly in individual stocks if the investment is handled through a custodial account.

- You must have earned income to contribute to a Roth IRA. This means that if you take a year off from work and receive no compensation, you are not able to contribute to a Roth IRA that year.

- There has been some discussion recently in government circles about raising contribution limits on the Roth IRA or replacing it altogether with either a Retirement Savings Account (RSA) or something similar that would function much like a Roth IRA. Regardless of what becomes of the Roth IRA, chances are that some version of it (taxed contributions, tax-free withdrawals) will always be available, and for that reason it is something everyone should consider investing in. For the latest developments on the Roth IRA and RSA, visit the 403(b)wise website at *www.403bwise.com*.

Are there any additional retirement plans available for teachers who run side businesses?

Yes. Several plans exist, but the Simplified Employ Pension IRA (SEP-IRA) may be the easiest way for the self-employed and owners of small companies to save additional money for retirement. To set up a SEP-IRA, contact a vendor of your choice. Most vendors offer SEP-IRA plans.

Further details on the Roth IRA can be found in IRS Publication 590, *Individual Retirement Arrangements*. Further details on the SEP-IRA can be found in IRS Publication 560, *Retirement Plans for Small Business*. These publications may be downloaded from the IRS website at *www.irs.gov*. They may also be obtained by calling 1-800-TAX-FORMS.

ROTH 403(B) COMING IN 2006

As part of the Economic Growth and Reconciliation Act (EGTRRA) of 2001, a Roth 403(b) is scheduled to become available in 2006. Similar to the Roth IRA, the Roth 403(b) will allow individuals to contribute after-tax dollars to an account that will grow tax-deferred. Withdrawal of contributions will never be taxed. Employees will have the option of directing contributions to either a regular 403(b) or a Roth 403(b), or some combination of the two plans. Total contribution to either or both plans will be $15,000 for 2006. More details on the Roth 403(b) will be forthcoming from the IRS. The website *www.403bwise.com* will post the latest information on Roth 403(b) as it becomes available.

Go to the website *www.house.gov/rules/1836cr.pdf* to read the full text of EGTRRA.

INSURANCE BENEFITS

It is easy to overlook the value and necessity of insurance in wealth building. But, in fact, it may make sense to view insurance as a wealth-preserving tool. A retirement nest egg can soon disappear if it must be tapped to cover the costs of an illness or to replace income that has been lost to a disability. The good news is that many K–12 school districts and college and universities offer generous health insurance packages. In many cases, this benefit covers an entire family. In some cases, like that of Lynda, the retired teacher profiled in Chapter Three, teachers are granted health insurance benefits for life. But the soaring cost of health care (specifically, rising deductibles and the expense of adding family members to policies when employers eliminate automatic coverage for them) make scenarios like Lynda's less common. What follows is a list of critical protections that all families should have or should consider adding. Some of these policies and services are offered by the employer or are offered at a reduced rate. Disability insurance, in particular, can be quite expensive when purchased individually. Many employers use their purchasing power (i.e. numerous employees) to attain affordable disability insurance for their employees. Many employers also make available term life insurance for a nominal cost.

Wise wealth-preserving moves

- *Life insurance*
  What would you do if a loved one, particularly the main bread winner passed away? How would you pay the mortgage and the bills? Like investment products, there exist a myriad of

life insurance options (whole life, variable life, term life, etc.) Consider getting simple term insurance. With this product, you pay a low monthly premium (often as little as $12 per month for the young) and receive payment only if the covered person dies.

- *Disability insurance*
  What happens if you become disabled and are not capable of working? Your most valuable asset may be your ability to earn money. What happens if this is suddenly taken away? Again, how would you pay the mortgage and the bills? Some employers provide disabilty insurance, some do not. Does yours? Get disability insurance, either through your employer or on your own.

- *Long-term care insurance*
  The chance of needing long-term care medical service has been estimated to be around 40%. Nursing home costs are astronomical and rising. Investigate coverage when you turn 40 while premiums are still relatively low.

- *Property, casualty, auto, and umbrella insurance*
  Do you have enough? It may be wise to purchase these policies separately or through more than one agent to ensure you have the best coverage of each.

- *Will, trust, and Power of Attorney*
  What will happen to your assets when you pass? Have you appointed a guardian for your children in the event of death? Who will make the medical decisions for you if you become incapacitated? Hire an attorney who specializes in this field

to draft these documents. Do not rely on computer software, the Internet, or boilerplate material for these critical legal documents.

HOMEWORK: Visit the benefits department at your employer. Find out exactly what insurance options and policies are available to you, and the cost of each. Next, visit the *insure.com* website to get more information about insurance products and cost. Find out how much it costs to get $500,000 of term life insurance in the state in which you reside. Another sound source of information on insurance and other important money and consumer matters is the Consumer Reports website (*www.consumerreports.org*). Viewing premium content at the site is subject to a fee, but there is a discount for subscribers to *Consumer Reports* magazine. A trip to your library will allow you to read back issues of *Consumer Reports* for free. Next, visit *www.ambest.com* and *www.moodys.com* to check the independent ratings of various insurance companies. Finally, call three attorneys and ask for information and pricing on preparing a Will, a trust, and Power of Attorney paperwork. Armed with all of this information, you can take steps to protect yourself and your loved ones.

CHAPTER SIX

Get Your Assets in Gear: Understanding Assets and Benchmarks

"The safest way to double your money is to fold it over and put it in your pocket." — Kin Hubbard

Now that you have a working knowledge of the wealth-building tools—pensions, 403(b)s, 457(b)s, and Roth IRAs—that are available, it would be helpful for you to become familiar with assets and benchmarks before you begin investing.

WHAT IS AN ASSET CLASS?

In its simplest form, the term "asset class" refers to securities that have similar features. The three major asset classes are cash, stocks, and bonds.

What is cash?

Cash is an asset that can be immediately converted into dollars without potential for a loss. Checking accounts and money-market accounts are considered cash accounts.

What is a stock?

A stock is an ownership share in a company that allows you to participate in any gains or losses realized by the company. You actually own a small piece of the company in which you hold stock (proportional to the number of shares you own). Stocks are sometimes referred to as equities.

Stocks by size

- Large-cap (over $15 billion in market capitalization)
  EXAMPLE: General Electric Co.
- Mid-cap (between $2 billion and $15 billion in market capitalization)
  EXAMPLE: Office Depot
- Small-cap (under $2 billion in capitalization).
  EXAMPLE: Getty Images, Inc.

> To calculate the market capitalization of a company, multiply the number of distributed shares by the company's price per share.

History has shown that the smaller the stock, the higher the expected return (gain). History has also shown, however, that the smaller the stock, the more it will fluctuate in value (potentially magnifying the loss or gain).

Stocks by character—value and growth

Character, as it relates to stocks, refers to how a stock is classified against its peers. Two basic classifications exist: value and growth. Companies do not always stay in the same category; a growth stock can become a value stock, and vice versa.

Growth — A financially solid company with demonstrated strong growth potential. Wal-Mart and Microsoft are classic growth companies.

Value — An out-of-favor company whose stock price is distressed. During the late 1970s Chrysler was under duress and the value of its stock fell accordingly.

Blend — A company with characteristics of both growth and value.

What is a bond?

A bond is a form of debt issued by a governmental entity or a company. When you invest in a bond, you are lending money. In return you are paid interest. Bonds can be segregated by credit quality and maturity.

73

Bonds by credit quality

Credit quality refers to the ability of the company or governmental entity to pay back its bondholders. The two major types of credit quality are investment grade and noninvestment grade. Investment grade refers to those companies or governmental entities that have a solid history of paying their bills and have sufficient assets to pay bills in the future. These entities will be able to borrow at a lower interest rate because there is less chance of default. Noninvestment grade companies have either missed interest payments in the past or do not have sufficient assets to meet interest payments in the future. These entities will have to pay a higher rate of interest in order to attract investors because a greater chance of default exists. Noninvestment grade bonds may be referred to as high-yield or junk bonds.

Bonds by maturity

Bonds are like kids—some are very immature. Just kidding! Every bond has an expiration date or maturity. With the purchase of a bond, you are accepting a promise to be paid interest until some point in the future when the organization issuing the bond will pay you back your original investment. Bond maturity can be classified into three basic categories:

- Long term: fifteen to thirty years
- Intermediate: five to fifteen years
- Short term: one to five years

When you purchase a bond (or bond fund), you should be aware of the maturity period. Academic research has shown that you rarely are rewarded for the extra risk you incur when purchasing a longer-term bond. Long-term bonds pay higher interest rates, but their prices fluctuate more because of changes in interest rates. It is important to note that an inverse relationship exists between interest rates and bond fund prices. When interest rates rise, bond fund prices will decline. When interest rates decline, bond fund prices will rise. Consequently, the optimal maturity period is somewhere between one and five years.

Before looking at benchmarks, it is important that you become familiar with two more terms: fixed investments and mutual funds.

What is a fixed investment?

A fixed investment is a relatively safe investment—such as a certificate of deposit, a money-market account, a fixed annuity, or a short-term bond fund—that yields a steady, fixed payout.

What is a mutual fund?

A mutual fund is an investment that pools money from many
investors and invests the money in stocks, bonds, cash, or some
combination of the three. For more information on mutual funds,
see Chapter Seven.

WHAT IS A BENCHMARK?

A benchmark is a standard by which something is measured.
For investing purposes, the two most popular standards of
measurement are the Standard and Poor's 500 (S&P 500) and the
Dow Jones Industrial Average. Individual stocks go up and down
every day, but most investors want to know the overall direction
of the market or of a segment of the market. The S&P 500
basically represents the 500 largest companies in the U.S. When
this benchmark (or index) rises or falls, investors have an idea of
the overall direction of the U.S. market. The Dow Jones Industrial
Average, the oldest investment benchmark (or index), is made up
of thirty well-known American companies that represent a cross
section of industries, including aerospace, automobiles, energy,
entertainment, financial services, medical, retail, technology,
and telecommunications. Companies that are a part of the Dow
include American Express, Boeing, Coca Cola, ExxonMobil, General
Electric, Merck, Walt Disney, and Wal-Mart.

Other popular stock indexes

The Wilshire 5000 tracks all publicly traded American stocks. It
is the broadest indicator of the overall market and may provide an
even more accurate market snapshot than the S&P 500 does. This

index is also known as the total stock market index.

The Russell 2000 gauges the performance of American small companies.

The MSCI-EAFE measures the performance of twenty developed overseas markets, including Europe, Australia, and the Far East.

Numerous mutual funds that mirror specific indexes are available to investors. Known as index funds, these funds typically have very low expenses because they require little active management. Index investing, often called passive investing, is covered in Chapter Eleven.

Popular bond indexes

The Lehman short term government/credit index tracks government and corporate short-term bonds with maturities of one to five years.

The Lehman intermediate term government/credit index gauges government and corporate medium-term bonds with maturities of five to ten years.

The Lehman long term government/credit index tracks government and corporate long-term bonds with maturities of twenty to thirty years.

The Lehman aggregate bond index is made up of government, corporate, and mortgage-backed bonds with average maturity of five to ten years. This represents the total bond universe of public investment-grade bonds in the U.S.

The worst year for bond returns is usually better than the worst year for stock returns, meaning that bonds are, by nature, less volatile and safer investment than stocks. According to Vanguard, across the broad markets during the past thirty years, stocks' worst twelve-month period was from October 1973 to September 1974, when the Wilshire 5000 Index returned –41.5%. The bond market's worst twelve months over the past thirty years, as represented by the total return from the Lehman aggregate bond index, was a tamer –9.2% from April 1979 through March 1980.

HOMEWORK: Purchase a daily newspaper and turn to the business or financial section. Locate information on the performance of the S&P 500 and other benchmarks. This section is often titled "Major Stock Indexes" or "Major Indexes." Become familiar with this section. Study not only daily performance of the indexes but also year-to-date information and five and ten year returns. Share what you learned with at least two colleagues.

CHAPTER SEVEN

Where to Stash the Cash: A Look at Fixed Annuities, Variable Annuities, and Mutual Funds

"When money talks, nobody notices what grammar it uses."

— Anonymous

When it comes to investing in 403(b) and 457(b) plans, investors typically have three main investing options:

1. *Fixed annuity contracts with insurance companies*
   These are sometimes referred to as tax-sheltered annuities (TSA) or tax-deferred annuities (TDA).

2. *Variable annuity contracts with insurance companies*
   These are also sometimes called tax-sheltered annuities.

3. *A custodial account made up of mutual funds*
   This is known as a 403(b)(7) account.

NOTE: In addition to the above options, Roth IRA investors have the ability to invest in individual stocks.

Annuities

An annuity is a contract with an insurance company. There are two kinds of annuities, fixed and variable, and there are two phases to an annuity, the accumulation phase and the distribution phase. This section will focus on the accumulation stage, while Chapter Fourteen focuses on the distribution stage.

Agent services

Annuities are typically sold by agents who can and do provide valuable services. The key is to figure out exactly what services you are receiving, and exactly what fees you are paying for these services. Only then can you determine the true value of using an agent. For more details on using an agent or advisor, see the Seventh Commandment in Chapter Eleven.

FIXED ANNUITIES

While fixed annuities come in many flavors, the three most common are the traditional fixed annuity, the two-tier annuity, and the equity-indexed annuity.

Fees

There is no set fee for a fixed annuity. Annuity fees are built into the product in the same way that a bank makes money on a certificate of deposit (CD). EXAMPLE: The annuity company may believe they can earn 6 percent on an investment, so they will pay you 4 percent. The company makes its money on the difference; in this example that difference is 2 percent.

Traditional fixed annuity

In a traditional fixed annuity, you are usually given two interest rates: the current rate and the guaranteed rate. The current rate is the return the insurance company promises for a set period of time, typically one to five years. Returns on the current rate generally average from 4 percent to 6 percent. The guaranteed rate is the rate that you will receive after your current rate expires, regardless of market conditions. Guaranteed rates usually run between 2 percent and 3 percent. A traditional annuity is similar to a bank CD, but it does not contain the FDIC guarantee against loss. Seek products that offer a decent rate of return, come with limited or no surrender periods, and have clear, easy-to-understand rules of operation.

Two-tier annuity

Perhaps a better name for this product would be the 100-tear annuity. The two-tier annuity sports high commissions and long surrender periods. This annuity forces the investor to annuitize (agree to a locked in payout schedule) in order to avoid surrender charges. The pitch to the prospective customer typically works like this: the going rate for annuities is 4.5 percent, but an insurance company will advertise an annuity paying a 6 percent rate. Sounds like a good deal. However, the fine print states that unless you annuitize during a set period of time, the rate reverts to 3 percent. If you do annuitize during this set time period, you will have locked yourself into the company's annuitization schedule (which may pay only 2.5 percent or less during the payment phase). If you decide you want flexibility and decline to annuitize, you are usually stuck with the obligation to pay permanent surrender charges. If you choose to exit the annuity altogether, the penalties are especially stiff. Avoid this product.

81

Equity-index annuity

How would you like an investment that offers the growth of the stock market with none of the risk? Who wouldn't jump at this opportunity? Better look before you leap, however.

Equity-index annuities (EIA) and the insurance agents who peddle them have invaded the 403(b) market. What is an EIA? Quite simply, it is a fixed annuity whose annual return is linked to a specific market index—the S&P 500, for example. If the index rises, you are credited with interest. If it falls, you are credited either with nothing or with a specified minimum rate.

Lack of disclosure, complicated return formulas, extremely high commissions, and long surrender periods have all combined to make this product a riddle wrapped in an enigma. Avoid it at all costs. Insurance companies have purposely made it complicated to hide the fact that it does not deliver what it purports. Investors do not participate in dividends (which historically have made up about 4 percent of the market's return over time). In other words, investors are not able to participate in the total return of the market. When all is said and done figure on an actual return in the range of 3 percent to 5 percent. Historically, the market (as judged by the S&P 500) has returned about 11 percent over time (before inflation, fees, and taxes), a far cry from the 3 percent to 5 percent that you will receive. The enticement here is that you appear to be taking the risk of the market, when in reality you are taking the risk of a fixed annuity. Over time you will receive the return of a fixed annuity—or worse. New products are always coming onto the market, and someday an EIA that provides investors with the potential growth of the market without the risk may, in fact, arrive. But don't bet on it.

Note on bonus annuities

This product adds an additional 3 percent to 6 percent interest rate to your initial contract as a "bonus" for signing up or extending an existing annuity. Sounds enticing. Beware. The bonus annuity is typically nothing more than a gimmick. The bonus usually lasts for only one year. To compensate for this bonus in the first year, the interest rate is reduced in later years. Bonus annuities typically come with long surrender periods and high surrender penalties. Avoid these products.

Fixed annuity caveats

83

If you decide to purchase an annuity, it is critical that you check out the insurance company's rating. Teachers will appreciate the A+ to F rating system. It is unwise to purchase an annuity from a company with a rating lower than an A. Remember that a guarantee is only as good as the company backing it. Independent ratings of insurance companies are available from A.M. Best (*www.ambest.com*) and Moody's (*www.moodys.com*). Rating information can also be found at *www.insure.com* and *www.annuity.com*.

VARIABLE ANNUITIES

Variable annuities are basically mutual funds wrapped in an insurance package. A variable annuity ties its return to the performance of one or more mutual funds that invest in stocks and/or bonds and/or cash holdings. These investments are often referred to as subaccounts. The value of the investment will vary (hence, the term "variable") depending on the performance of the investments in the subaccounts.

It has been said that variable annuities are sold, rather than bought. One of the salesperson's favorite selling points is that earnings in an annuity, both fixed and variable, grow tax-deferred. This is true. However, since 403(b) and 457(b) plans are, by design, tax-deferred plans, you derive no further benefit from choosing an annuity product.

It has also been said that investing your retirement plan money in variable annuity products is akin to using an umbrella indoors. Unless you own a leaky home in Seattle or the Brazilian rain forest, proceed with the utmost caution. In fact, the National Association of Variable Annuities (NAVA) preaches this very sentiment. In a March 2004 appearance on CNNfn's Your Money program, a NAVA representative said that annuities are right only for people who have contributed the maximum to a 401(k) and other similar plan. The 403(b) and 457(b) are such plans. Which begs this question: if the national voice of the variable annuity industry urges investors to consider variable annuities only outside of their tax-deferred retirement plans, why would employers even allow such products to be offered inside 403(b) and 457(b) plans?

Fee-only financial planners will tell you that few investors are candidates for variable annuities under any circumstances. "I think variable annuities are oversold and underexplained," says planner Laura Tarbox, of Tarbox Equity, whose firm manages more than $115 million for clients. This sentiment is echoed by Gary Schatsky, president of the ObjectiveAdvice Group and a fee-only NAPFA Registered Financial Advisor. He says that annuities usually only make sense outside of retirement plans for a very select group of wealthy investors who are in a high tax bracket and have a significant amount of cash they need to tie up.

The notable exception to the no-annuity school of thought is the insurance company TIAA-CREF (Teachers Insurance & Annuity Association/College Retirement Equity Funds), the largest holder of pension assets in the world. With fees that are among the lowest in the financial services industry and an absence of surrender charges, an annuity product from TIAA-CREF can be just as wise a choice as a low cost, no-load mutual fund.

Fees

High fees are what make most variable annuities a poor investment choice. The following are the most common fees.

Mortality and expense (M&E) component

A popular selling point of variable annuities is the insurance, or death, benefit (known as the mortality component). This feature ensures that heirs will not receive less than what was contributed to the account. The death benefit typically works like this: the beneficiary (spouse, child, etc.) will receive the greater of (1) all the money in the account or (2) some greater guaranteed minimum (such as all purchase payments minus prior withdrawals).

EXAMPLE: You own a variable annuity that offers a death benefit equal to the total purchase payments (minus withdrawals). You have made purchase payments totaling $50,000, but investment losses have brought your account's value to $45,000. According to the Securities and Exchange

Commission, if you die, your designated beneficiary will receive the total contributed ($50,000), even though the value of the account is now only $45,000.

To receive this benefit, of course, you must die. While the market does, indeed, fall from time to time, the market (as judged by the S&P 500) has historically returned about 11 percent before inflation, fees, and taxes. Figure that the death benefit (M&E) will cost you about 1.25 percent in fees a year (the majority of this fee goes to agent commissions). That might seem like a minuscule number, but it is not. Over thirty years this "benefit" can erode more than 23 percent in potential returns—meaning tens of thousands of lost dollars. Over forty years your potential returns could be reduced by more than 31 percent. Two things must happen for this "benefit" to make any sense: first, you must die. Second, your investment must have lost money. Let us say you die and your investment has not lost money. You are now dead, and you have paid for an insurance feature that your beneficiaries will not even receive. Even if you die, and the market goes down, there is a cheaper way to ensure that your beneficiaries are taken care of: term life insurance. Recall from Chapter Five that this is extremely affordable insurance that pays if and only if you die during coverage. If an agent pushes the necessity of the M&E "protection," ask him or her two questions: Do you yourself invest in products that have an M&E component? And do you have statistics on the number of deceased participants whose survivors benefited from the M&E? At the end of the day only you can decide the true value of the M&E expense. If it gives you a greater sense of security, and you understand the costs associated with it, then it can make sense for your individual situation.

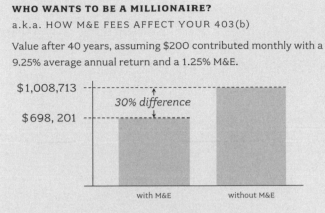

WHO WANTS TO BE A MILLIONAIRE?

a.k.a. HOW M&E FEES AFFECT YOUR 403(b)

Value after 40 years, assuming $200 contributed monthly with a 9.25% average annual return and a 1.25% M&E.

30% difference

$1,008,713

$698, 201

with M&E   without M&E

NOTE: This chart is presented for illustrative purposes only and does not reflect actual performance, or predict future results, of any investment account.

Riders

Additional insurance "benefits" that are dubious as well as expensive include step-ups and living benefits, among others. Rider expenses can range from 0.25 percent to 1.25 percent, in effect doubling the cost of your variable annuity.

Subaccount

According to Morningstar, the average management fee for a variable annuity subaccount (the mutual fund within in the variable annuity) is 0.82 percent. This primarily covers the manager's compensation, research, and other staff expenses.

Policy charge

For accounts under $50,000, the insurance company typically charges an annual fee of $30. This charge is designed to offset the cost of maintaining accounts with low balances.

Trading costs

Trading costs are never disclosed, yet they can add significantly to the price you pay for an investment. Managers of subaccounts incur additional expenses related to the buying and selling of securities (stock and bonds). These expenses can easily add an additional 1 percent in costs.

Fees, with the exception of trading costs, are disclosed in the prospectus (or information booklet) that is required to accompany a variable annuity investment. This information is often available online as well.

TYPICAL VARIABLE ANNUITY COSTS		
M&E	1.25%	
Riders	0 to 1.25%	
Subaccount	0.25 to 2.00%	
Policy charge		$0 to 50
Trading costs	0.20 to 2.00%	
Range of costs	1.70 to 6.50%	+ $0 to 50

Annuity surrender periods and charges

"Put your hands up and nobody gets hurt!" Or more accurately, leave an annuity early, and you get hurt. This is because annuities—both fixed annuities and variable annuities—almost always carry surrender charges. This means that if you decide to move your money into another investment, you will incur a penalty. Even if you keep the money under the umbrella of your 403(b) plan or 457(b) plan (meaning that your intentions are not to get your hands on the money), you must still pay the fiddler. And fiddling lessons are not cheap. Often lasting seven to ten years (and in some cases up to twenty years), surrender penalties claim a percentage of your balance. Surrender penalties typically begin at 7 percent (or higher) of balance and decline one percentage per year. EXAMPLE: If you wish to move your money after Year Two, you may owe 5 percent of the balance; after Year Three, your penalty would be 4 percent of the balance, and so on, until after Year Seven you finally owe no penalty.

Also keep in mind that some annuity products impose rolling surrender charges that kick in with each new contribution. This means that the most recent contribution you make is locked into a seven-year "surrender jail." Do not expect time off for good behavior!

Surrender charges typically exist for two reasons: to compensate the agent selling the annuity and to lock you into a relationship with a financial company.

89

MUTUAL FUNDS

A mutual fund is an investment that pools money from many investors and invests in stocks, bonds, cash, or some combination of the three. The combined holdings of stocks, bonds or other assets the fund owns are known as its portfolio. Each investor in the fund owns shares, which represent a part of these holdings. The benefits of a mutual fund are lower costs, greater diversification, and professional management. After all, it would be very expensive for an individual to buy hundreds of stocks and bonds and then employ a professional manager to oversee these investments.

Mutual funds come in all shapes, sizes and costs. Some are small in size; some are large. Some invest in a few stocks; some in thousands. Some buy large-company stocks, while others buy small-company stocks. Some charge a commission; some do not. All mutual funds have one thing in common: mutual ownership.

Most mutual funds are "actively managed." A manager (or team of managers) selects investments believed to be appropriate. Some mutual funds, however, are "passively managed." This is also known as index investing; these mutual funds simply make purchases that mirror investment benchmarks like the S&P 500 or the Wilshire 5000. Index funds are known for their low fees.

Load and no-load

Two kinds of mutual funds exist: loaded mutual funds and no-load mutual funds. A load is a commission that the investor must pay in order to purchase a fund. No-load mutual funds charge no commissions. Load or no load, all mutual funds have operating costs—and in the end it is these operating costs, along with performance and diversification (explained in Chapter Eight), that investors should focus on.

Share classes—alphabet soup

Loaded mutual funds, which charge a commission, come in a variety of share classes—A, B, C, D, F, I, S, T, and Y. Confused? It is easy to be. Each of these shares represents a different way of paying for your mutual fund. While there are many different share classes, the most common are A, B, and C. What follows is a basic explanation of each.

Class A share

Class A shares charge a front-end load (that is, a commission). In this structure, you pay an up-front commission that reduces your initial investment. EXAMPLE: If you purchase $100 worth of class A shares with a 5 percent load, you will pay a $5 commission. So, your investment (or principal) is immediately reduced to $95. This fee is in addition to the annual operating expenses which all funds charge. However, annual operating expenses are usually lower in A shares than in other loaded funds. Over time, A shares are probably the cheapest class of commissioned-based shares if held long-term.

Some programs offer A shares without a front-end load. Be sure to check for other fees that may be associated with the product.

91

Class B shares

Class B shares allow your entire principal to go to work immediately. However, operating expenses are much higher for B shares than for A shares. Furthermore, if you sell before a specified time period, usually four to seven years, you will owe a surrender penalty of up to 7 percent of your balance (referred to as contingent deferred sales charge). This structure was developed as a way to put your entire principal to work immediately, while ensuring that your broker gets compensated immediately as well. Surrender fees are put in place to cover the commission advanced to the broker in the event the investor exits the fund early. Because of the need to cover the cash advance to the broker, expenses in B shares usually run almost twice as high as in A shares. Typically, a B share will convert to an A share in seven to ten years.

Class C shares

Class C shares give you the most flexibility, but at a cost. There is no up-front sales charge with a C share, and you usually need only hold the fund for a year before you are free to sell it. However, C shares normally do not convert to A shares, making them the most expensive of the three share classes when held over the long term.

A broker has the duty to ensure that you are in the mutual-fund share class that, given your financial situation and investment goals, benefits you the most. If you are purchasing a mutual fund from a commissioned salesperson, make sure that you understand what share class you are being offered and why. Be certain that you are in the share class that benefits you, not the broker.

No-load mutual funds

No matter the name—A, B, C, or D—many investors are giving loaded mutual funds a big fat F. Increasingly, investors are choosing to invest in no-load mutual funds, which charge no up-front commissions. No-load mutual funds earn their money though management fees that can generally range from 0.15 percent to more than 2 percent. The industry average, according to fund tracker Morningstar, is about 1.4 percent.

Fees

The following are common costs associated with mutual fund ownership. Not all funds charge all of these fees.

Expense ratio (or operating expenses) — These are charges for investment management, research, administration, and distribution services.

12b-1 fee — This charge generally compensates brokers, with a payment to the representative who sold the fund. It can also cover marketing costs.

Trading costs — Mutual funds may incur additional expenses related to the buying and selling of individual securities (stock and bonds). These expenses can easily add an additional 1 percent in costs.

Custodial fee — This is a charge for safekeeping or physically holding the securities in a fund. This fee may be waived once a certain account balance is reached.

Wrap account fee — This is a fee charged by brokerage firms to cover investment advice. This fee usually starts at 1.5 percent of assets and drops as your account balance increases. This charge is in addition to the expense ratio of your mutual fund.

SUMMARY OF TYPICAL MUTUAL FUND COSTS		
Expense ratio	0.15 to 1.40%	
12b-1 fee	0 to 1.00%	
Trading costs	0.20 to 2.00%	
Custodial fee		$0 to 50
Wrap fee	0 to 1.50%	
Range of costs	*0.35 to 5.59%* +	*$0 to 50*

403(b)(7) custodial account

Mutual funds were added as an investment option for the 403(b) in 1974. If you choose to invest 403(b) money directly into a mutual fund, as opposed to investing in a mutual fund that is part of a variable annuity subaccount, then you are investing in a 403(b)(7) custodial account. The mutual fund company is acting as the account custodian.

In the thirty years since mutual funds became an investment option, less than 20 percent of 403(b) money has been invested in mutual funds. This compares, according to the Spectrem Group, to the more than 80% of 401(k)-plan money that is directed into mutual funds. Reasons abound to explain why 403(b) participants fail to use mutual funds as their investment vehicle of choice. The insurance industry (and its sales force) has become so ingrained in the 403(b) market that it is often very difficult for mutual fund companies, especially those that specialize in low-fee products, to make headway. The Los Angeles Unified School District, the nation's largest, currently has more than 150 vendors, most of which are annuity products. In order to stand out in such a crowded field, vendors are almost forced to hire agents to promote products. Such an approach drives up costs. It is interesting to note that 401(k) plans typically only offer mutual funds.

Another culprit is lack of knowledge by employers. Many employers simply do not understand how the 403(b) works and have basically farmed out responsibility of the plan to the vendors. If proposed changes to the 403(b) become reality in 2006, employers are going to be required to take more responsibility for their 403(b) plans.

Mutual-fund caveats

Cost — Academic studies have shown that no correlation exists between high-cost mutual funds and improved or superior performance. There is plenty of evidence, however, that high-cost funds will on average underperform the market. According to

Lipper Analytical Services, over the ten years that ended in June 2000, more than 80 percent of "general equity" mutual funds (meaning garden variety stock funds) underperformed the S&P 500—the major benchmark for stock mutual funds.

Low portfolio turnover — Turnover refers to the active buying and selling of investments within the fund. The more trading there is, the more costs there are. High turnover increases costs for fund owners. It should be noted that index funds typically have very little portfolio turnover.

Purity of objective — This simply means you do not want a large-company stock fund to be buying small-company stocks. Look for funds that stick to their objectives.

Consistency and reliability — Look for funds that are consistent with their style and performance. If large-cap growth stocks are up 20 percent, it is fair to expect your own large-cap growth fund to be up accordingly. Conversely, if large-cap growth stocks are down 20 percent, your large-cap growth fund should reflect that drop. Consistency of performance is a telltale sign that the manager is true to the fund's objective.

Questions to ask before you purchase an annuity

1. Ask to see the annuity contract, which details the rules of operation.
2. What is the length and return of the current rate?
3. What is the length and return of the guaranteed rate?
4. What is the cost and name of all fees, including commissions, in this product?
5. How will the fees affect my portfolio over time?

6. Why is this product being "sold" over another product?

7. How long is the surrender period and what is the penalty?

8. Why should I put 403(b) or 457(b) money into an annuity?

9. How is this a better investment than a no-load mutual fund?

10. How is the company rated by A.M. Best and Moody's?

Questions to ask before you purchase a variable annuity

1. Ask to see the variable annuity prospectus, the document that details cost, objective, risk, performance, and operating rules.

2. What is the annual operating expense of the sub-account investment?

3. What is the annual cost of the mortality and expense (M&E) component?

4. What are the names and costs of all fees, including commissions, in this product?

5. What is the total commission to all parties, including the sales representative?

6. How long is the surrender period and what is the penalty? Is there a rolling surrender schedule with this product?

7. How is this a better investment than a no-load mutual fund?

8. How do the subaccounts in this variable annuity fit into my overall portfolio?

9. What percentage of people who own variable annuities actually collect on the death benefit beyond the account value?

10. Is a living benefit being sold? If so, what is the rate guaranteed during annuitization?

11. How will the fees affect my portfolio over time?

12. Is this a bonus annuity? (If it is, run—do not walk—out of the meeting).

13. What is the advantage of using a tax-deferred vehicle (an annuity) in a tax-deferred plan—403(b) or 457(b) or Roth IRA, or a combination of these? (NOTE: There is no advantage.)

14. Do you have a special incentive to sell this product over another?

Questions to ask before purchasing a mutual fund

1. Ask to see the fund prospectus, the document that details cost, objective, risk, performance, and fund operating rules.

2. What are the names and costs of all fees, including commissions, in this product?

3. How does this fund fit into my overall portfolio?

4. How long is the surrender period and what is the penalty?

5. Is there a rolling surrender schedule with this fund?

6. How long has the current manager or management team been in place?

7. How does this fund's long-term performance compare to its benchmark?

8. How will the fees affect my portfolio over time?

9. Do you have a special incentive to sell this product over another?

HOMEWORK: Go to *www.sec.gov*, the website for the Securities and Exchange Commission. The primary mission of this agency is to protect investors and to maintain the integrity of the securities markets in the U.S. The SEC website contains a wealth of information for all investors, especially beginners. Go to the search box on the home page and alternately type in "annuity," "variable annuity," and "mutual fund." Your search will yield numerous easy-to-read stories on these subjects. Read several of each. Print one for each subject and share them with at least two of your colleagues.

CHAPTER EIGHT

How to Stash the Cash: Considering Risk Tolerance and Asset Allocation

"It's better to do nothing with your money than something you don't understand." — Suze Orman

No two investors are the same, but all investors should be aware of two critical components of investing before beginning: risk tolerance and asset allocation.

RISK TOLERANCE

How would you feel if the value of your investment portfolio dropped by 20 percent in one year? This is an entirely likely scenario, since the market experiences such a drop once every five years. As the following demonstrates, the stock market can be very risky in the short term.

From January 1970 to December 2003, according to KJE Computer Systems, which provides financial calculators for websites (*www.dinkytown.net*), the average compounded rate of return for the S&P 500 was approximately 11.7 percent per year. That is the good news. The bad news is the bouts of wild fluctuation in the market that occurred during that same period. During one twelve-month-period, the S&P 500 soared by an astonishing 64 percent. During another twelve-month period, the S&P 500 dropped by a gut-wrenching 39 percent. Wouldn't it have been great if you had entered the market just before the 64 percent one-year gain? Conversely, imagine your feelings if you had entered the market just prior to the 39 percent drop? The volatility of these two years should give all investors pause. However, for the long-term investor—which should describe all readers of this book, even those less than ten years from retirement—the most valuable piece of information is the average performance of the S&P 500 during the thirty-three-year period: an 11.7 percent average annual gain (before inflation, fees, and taxes). This is pretty impressive when you consider the record market decline of 1973–74, the recent technology stock meltdown, the attacks of September 11, and various other calamities that occurred over this extended period of time. The lesson here is that time has a way of smoothing out market fluctuations (and risk), which rewards the long-term investor.

> The past is no guarantee of future returns, but consider this: since 1802 stocks have never produced a negative inflation-adjusted return if held for twenty years or more.*

The bottom line, as it relates to risk tolerance, is that only you can decide what makes the most sense for your situation. You may feel more comfortable in a less volatile investment like a fixed annuity that guarantees 3 percent to 4 percent or a mutual fund that is more weighted toward safer fixed investments. While it may take you longer to accumulate savings and reach your savings goals, you cannot put a price on peace of mind.

---

* SOURCE: *The Average Family's Guide to Financial Freedom*, by Bill and Mary Toohey.

The wisest course of action is to educate yourself and to invest at your personal comfort level.

ASSET ALLOCATION

The second critical component of wise investing is asset allocation—the process of distributing investments across various asset classes (stocks, bonds, cash) in an attempt to moderate the inevitable ups and downs the market will experience. Not all areas of the market go up or down in lockstep. For instance, small-company stocks may soar in the same year that large-company stocks struggle. Bonds and fixed investments may do well for a period, while stocks struggle. To offset divergent performance, experts recommend that you own a portfolio (a collection of investments) spread among a variety of asset classes. This process is also referred to as diversification, and simply means "Don't put all of your eggs in one basket."

Investors must take steps not only to properly allocate their investments when they begin investing, but they must also adjust their allocation as savings goals change and as they near retirement. Unfortunately, studies indicate that investors are loath to make changes to asset allocation. Many investors retire with the same allocation they had on the day they began investing.* Such a scenario begs disaster. Why? Imagine being a year from retirement and your investments are completely in stock mutual funds. What happens if the market experiences a 20 percent drop? Or worse, the 39 percent decline that was described earlier? This is exactly what happened in the late

* SOURCE: *Save More Tomorrow: Using Behavioral Economics to Increase Employee Saving*, by Richard H. Thaler and Shlomo Benartzi.

1990s—a period that was marked by an "irrational exuberance" brought on by a soaring stock market. This foolish investing fever led many investors, including those close to retirement, to be invested almost entirely in stocks and stock mutual funds as they chased unsustainable performance. The result? Disaster. When the market came crashing down in 2000–02, many portfolios were whacked by losses of 30 percent or more because they were not diversified. Imagine being a year from retirement and watching your $300,000 portfolio plummet to $210,000 or less.

A popular school of thought is that the longer your investment horizon (that is, the longer you have until you need access to the money), the more weighted your portfolio should be toward stocks and stock funds. Conversely, the closer to retirement you are, the more your portfolio should be weighted toward fixed investments (bonds, CDs, money-market accounts, etc). The reason? The market can fluctuate widely in the short term, which can be very dangerous for those approaching retirement.

The needs of each investor are unique, but there is another rule of thumb that you should try to follow: the percentage of fixed investments in your portfolio should mirror your age. EXAMPLE: A forty-year-old might have a portfolio split 60 percent stock mutual funds and 40 percent fixed investments.

Two approaches to asset alloc ation

There are literally hundreds of approaches to asset allocation. This section will focus on two simple approaches that can be set up without the help of a financial professional.

APPROACH ONE: *Do-it-yourself allocation*

A classic allocation portfolio is represented in the chart below. It is split 60 percent stock mutual funds and 40 percent fixed investments. Notice that the stock portion is further allocated among small-company funds, large-company funds, and international funds, while the fixed portion is allocated between cash (typically money-markets) and other fixed investments (typically bond funds). Such an allocation has historically returned better than 8 percent (before fees and trading costs).

MODEL PORTFOLIO

The allocation represented below has historically returned better than 8 percent (before fees and trading costs).

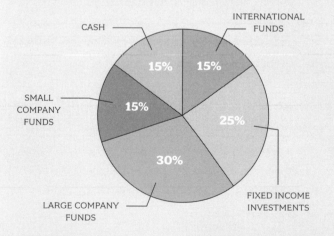

CASH — 15%
INTERNATIONAL FUNDS — 15%
SMALL COMPANY FUNDS — 15%
FIXED INCOME INVESTMENTS — 25%
LARGE COMPANY FUNDS — 30%

NOTE: This chart is presented for illustrative purposes only and does not reflect actual performance, or predict future results, of any investment account.

Since it is often difficult for investors to allocate investments on their own, many vendors offer a single static mutual fund that is allocated in a manner similar to this chart. This means that you do not have to select numerous investments on your own to achieve this allocation. The fund manager(s) regularly reallocate this one static fund to achieve its desired investment mix, which in this case is 60 percent stocks and 40 percent fixed investments. There are plenty of other fixed allocation funds with different mixes. EXAMPLE: A fund might be split 40 percent stocks and 60 percent fixed investments. Investors who are more aggressive might want a fund that is split 70 percent stocks and 30 percent fixed investments. Check with individual vendors for specific fund mixes.

While much simpler than allocating investments on your own, these single static funds still require you to take action if you want to change your allocation. EXAMPLE: You might have a single fixed mutual fund split 60 percent stocks and 40 percent fixed investments. As you approach retirement, you may prefer a more conservative mix—say 40 percent stocks and 60 percent fixed investments. To achieve a new mix, you must initiate change. This is not a difficult task, but as noted earlier most investors are loath to change their allocation mix. The next approach to asset allocation may have strong appeal for those who prefer an even more automatic approach.

APPROACH TWO: *Target-date funds*

It can often be difficult to allocate investments on your own, especially if you are just starting out and are contributing relatively small amounts. Plus, you must regularly monitor your allocation and adjust accordingly. For these reasons, mutual fund companies have devised single funds that are targeted at specific retirement dates and automatically adjust the allocation mix. Known by a variety of names—target-date funds, target-retirement funds, life cycle funds, and life strategy funds—these funds may be the simplest way to invest. Here is how they work:

1. An investor chooses an estimated retirement date, say 2018, and then picks a target-date fund that most closely corresponds to that date (EXAMPLE: a 2020 fund).
2. The longer the time horizon, the more weighted this type of fund is toward stocks. EXAMPLE: The T. Rowe Price 2030 fund is currently weighted 93 percent stocks and 7 percent fixed investments, while the T. Rowe Price 2010 fund is split 69 percent stocks and 31 percent fixed investments.
3. The fund gradually shifts to a more conservative allocation as the target retirement date approaches.
4. Investors simply contribute to one fund.
5. Retirement date funds at five-year increments from 2005 to 2045 are currently available.
6. There is some variation among vendors, but when the target date is reached, the fund remains open for about five years. During that time, its stock exposure is gradually reduced until its allocation mirrors that of a typical retirement fund (generally 80 percent fixed investments and a 20 percent mix of stocks). At that point the fund is rolled into a standard retirement fund operated by each vendor.

107

What also makes target-date funds so appealing is their low cost. There are plenty of target-date funds available that charge less than one percent in total fees. For beginning investors there may truly be no simpler or more affordable way to invest. Even for veteran investors these funds have a lot of appeal. NOTE: There is some asset-allocation variance in target-date funds among vendors. This means that some companies have a heavier stock to fixed investments mix than others. Some companies also employ actively managed funds in their target date lineup while others rely on index funds. For full details, consult individual vendors.

NOTE ON STOCKS AND FIXED INVESTMENTS: Historically, stocks give you the best chance of achieving your retirement goals. Why? The simplest explanation is that stocks and stock funds participate in profits, while bonds, bond funds, and fixed investments do not. This is not to say that an investor would be best served by a 100 percent stock allocation. On the contrary, fixed investments will steady a portfolio when the market declines, but fixed investments do not fully benefit when the market rises. Just as important, fixed investments are not as effective as stocks at countering the ravages of inflation (see the inflation gap chart in Chapter Fourteen). This all points to one essential conclusion: the investor who is properly allocated at all stages of the investing cycle—beginning, middle, and end—greatly increases his or her chance of reaching retirement goals.

CHAPTER NINE

A Short and Not-so-sweet Look at Fees

"Even though work stops, expenses run on." — Cato the Elder

As an investor you cannot predict how your investments will perform. Your only guide is past performance. The one aspect of investing that you can control, beyond picking what to invest in, is fees—what your individual investments cost. The number one factor determining your rate of return, after asset allocation, is fees. The chart below illustrates the enormous impact of fees on returns.

HOW FEES IMPACT RETURN

Value after 35 years, assuming $200 contributed monthly with an 8% average annual return.

		$548,750
	$409,585	
$336,320		
2.25% in fees	1.40% in fees	0.18% in fees
Average Variable Annuity	Average Managed Mutual Fund	Average Index Fund

NOTE: This chart is presented for illustrative purposes only and does not reflect actual performance, or predict future results, of any investment account.

SOURCE: Meridian Wealth Management (*www.meridianwealth.com*).

CHAPTER TEN

Charting Money Growth

"Time is on my side, yes it is." — Rolling Stones

The two best friends of any investor are compound interest and time. In fact, Albert Einstein called compound interest "the greatest mathematical discovery of all time." Compound interest simply means that you are earning interest (payment) not only on your principal (the balance of your investment) but on previously accrued interest. EXAMPLE: You invest $100 and earn $6 interest. You now have $106. Any new interest will now be based on an investment of $106 instead of on the previous $100. Obviously, the more money you have to invest and the longer you have to invest it, the more exponentially powerful the effect of compound interest.

Compound interest is a fun concept to teach students. One way I get the idea across is to share stories of my getting in trouble as a kid. I recount how I often was not content to merely get in trouble. Instead, I would "compound" my problem by fibbing or by some other such transgression. The result? Big trouble. This invariably leads to comments such as, "I know exactly what you mean!" and "Oh, man, Mr. Otter, that's nothing!"

The following charts demonstrate the power of compound interest and time by showing how much money you will need to save annually and monthly to reach different retirement savings goals. These numbers assume an 8 percent nominal rate of return;

these figures are for illustrative purposes only and do not reflect actual performance, or predict future results of any investment account. In saving for retirement it is important to note the erosive effects of inflation. A sum of $250,000 today will be worth less 20 years from now.

SAVINGS GOAL $250,000	Years until retirement	Must save annually	Must save monthly
	10	$17,257	$1,367
	15	$9,207	$722
	20	$5,463	$424
	25	$3,420	$263
	30	$2,207	$168
	35	$1,451	$109

SAVINGS GOAL $500,000	Years until retirement	Must save annually	Must save monthly
	10	$34,515	$2,733
	15	$18,415	$1,445
	20	$10,926	$849
	25	$6,839	$526
	30	$4,414	$335
	35	$2,902	$218

SAVINGS GOAL $1,000,000	Years until retirement	Must save annually	Must save monthly
	10	$69,029	$5,466
	15	$36,830	$2,890
	20	$21,852	$1,698
	25	$13,679	$1,051
	30	$8,827	$671
	35	$5,803	$436

SOURCE: Meridian Wealth Management (*www.meridianwealth.com*).

Saving a little bit early on can add up to much more than saving a lot later. Confused? Let us compare two investors: Timely Tina and Procrastinating Pete. Both Timely Tina and Procrastinating Pete are excellent, dedicated educators. Both care deeply about making a positive impact on their students. Both begin teaching at age twenty-five. But only Timely Tina starts a Roth IRA at this time. She begins dutifully contributing $3,000 annually. Ten years later, Procrastinating Pete finally gets around to starting a Roth IRA. He also dutifully contributes $3,000 a year. Let us assume that each earns an 8 percent annual return on their investment. And let us also assume that Timely Tina stops contributing at age thirty-five.

113

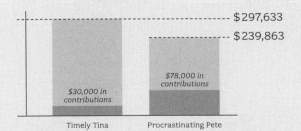

TIMELY TINA V. PROCRASTINATING PETE

End value of the Roth IRAs of Timely Tina and Procrastinating Pete at the time of retirement, assuming an 8% annual return. Timely Tina contributed $3,000 annually for only 10 years beginning at age 25. Procrastinating Pete contributed $3,000 annually for 26 years, but did not begin contributions until age 35.

$297,633

$239,863

$78,000 in contributions

$30,000 in contributions

Timely Tina   Procrastinating Pete

NOTE: This chart is presented for illustrative purposes only and does not reflect actual performance, or predict future results, of any investment account.

SOURCE: Meridian Wealth Management (*www.meridianwealth.com*).

Despite investing only $30,000 and contributing for only ten years, Timely Tina amassed $57,770 more than Procrastinating Pete, who contributed sixteen years longer. How can this be? Time—and the effects of compounding. It has been said that time waits for no one, and nowhere is this more true than when it comes to investing.

CHAPTER ELEVEN

The Teach and Retire Rich Commandments

"Say what you want about the Ten Commandments, you must always come back to the pleasant fact that there are only ten of them." — H.L. Mencken

THE FIRST COMMANDMENT
Begin today

You might be able to find a great substitute teacher for your class when you take ill, but as described in the previous chapter, when it comes to investing, there is no substitute for time.

THE SECOND COMMANDMENT
Pay yourself first

This may seem a strange concept. Teachers typically work for an employer who pays them, but as we learned in Chapter Four from *The Richest Man in Babylon*, "A part of all you earn is yours to keep." Many folks forget this concept. They pay everyone else first: the mortgage company, the telephone company, the electric company, and so on. This book is not advocating that you neglect paying those bills. On the contrary, timely payment of bills is wise money management. However, too many people pay themselves last. More often than not, this means that they do not pay themselves at all. Paying yourself first simply means that you contribute to retirement accounts and savings accounts at the beginning of the month. When you wait until the end of the month to contribute to your Roth IRA or other saving account, you may not have any money left to contribute. The good news is that contributions to defined-benefit plans (pension plans) and defined-contribution plans—403(b) and 457(b) plans—occur automatically. Investments in a Roth IRA, however, can be made at anytime, which makes this option dangerous for those who are inclined to procrastinate. Take the hassle out of investing by setting up automatic contributions from your paycheck or your bank account to your savings account, be it a Roth IRA, college savings account, holiday savings account, or even a travel savings fund. Vendors are only too happy to help you set up automatic investments.

THE THIRD COMMANDMENT
Invest in no-load products

As was explained earlier, there is a veritable alphabet soup of loaded mutual-fund share classes: A, B, C, D, to name a few. Confused? You should be. And that is how the investment industry prefers it. Such confusion requires that you use their "expertise" to navigate the mutual-fund jungle that the industry itself created. Give all loaded products a big fat "F" and proceed directly to no-load mutual funds and no-load annuities.

THE FOURTH COMMANDMENT
Get passive about investing

According to Warren Buffett, considered by many to be the savviest investor ever, "a very low cost—and I underscore low cost—index fund is probably going to be a very decent investment for the average investor, and it will do better than the average fund, where the fees are much higher."

Passive investing does not mean that you let yourself get pushed around by so-called financial professionals. The passive approach means spending a lot of time on the couch watching TV. Just kidding! But this image is an indication of how relaxed most passive investors feel. There are basically two approaches to mutual fund investing: active and passive.

1. *Active mutual fund investing*

   The active approach involves trusting a manager or team of managers, who strive to beat the market by what they hope are superior stock-picking skills. This involves active buying and selling of stocks. With the active approach to investing, the opportunity exists to beat the market. Recall from Chapter Seven, however, that most actively managed funds fail to beat the market.

2. *Passive mutual fund investing*

   The second approach to investing, the passive approach, (also known as index investing), does not strive to beat the market. Instead, it simply seeks to equal it. Historically, the overall market has returned on average about 11 percent annually (before inflation, fees, and taxes). This is a fairly good return. Especially when you consider that numerous index funds exist to mirror various segments of the market: the S&P 500, the Wilshire 5000, and so on. Since investments decisions are automatic and transactions are infrequent, the expenses of index funds tend to be much lower than

TEACH AND RETIRE RICH

those of actively managed funds. According to Morningstar, the average actively managed mutual fund charges about 1.4 percent in fees, while most index funds charge less than 0.5 percent annually. Why gamble that a high-fee fund is going to beat the market when you can spend as little as 0.2 percent and invest in Vanguard's Total Stock Market Index fund or something similar and be guaranteed of mirroring the market?

THE FIFTH COMMANDMENT
Invest with quality companies

The following companies are known for low fees and quality offerings: Dimensional Fund Advisors (typically only available through a financial advisor), Fidelity (no-load offerings), T. Rowe Price, TIAA-CREF, Vanguard, and USAA. You can locate their websites through a simple Internet search.

THE SIXTH COMMANDMENT
Fight for better investment choices at work

What if quality companies are not available in your 403(b) and 457(b) plans? This is a very real possibility at many K–12 employers. The first course of action is the frontal assault. Simply ask your employer to add better choices. Make them aware of how fees affect returns. Use information from this book. Heck, buy them a copy or three. Since your benefits officers are also plan participants, it is in their interest to have the best possible plan.

If all else fails, you may want to simply invest in a Roth IRA with the financial institution of your own choosing (the Roth IRA is explained in Chapter Five). After setting up a Roth IRA, you may then focus on getting your employer to wise up about 403(b) and 457(b) accounts. Good luck!

THE SEVENTH COMMANDMENT
Seek wise financial counsel

You do not need an agent or financial planner to set up or help you make contributions to a 403(b), 457(b), or Roth IRA. With financial education, patience, and realistic expectations, individuals are perfectly capable of managing these investments on their own. However, having said that, your wisest investment of all might be employing the services of a sage planner. The reason? Wise money stewardship is much more than managing a few investment accounts. A qualified planner can help get your entire financial house in order—tax planning, estate planning, retirement, insurance, college savings, etc. Due diligence, however, is the order of the day. Just as you would not blindly choose an investment (who among us has ever done that?), neither should you haphazardly choose a financial planner. To do so can have costly consequences. Complicating matters is the fact that just about anyone can call themselves a financial planner. Many have little experience, little knowledge, and little business calling themselves financial planners. If you are in the market for a planner do yourself a favor and hire a certified financial planner (CFP) who is paid on an hourly basis. CFP is the most recognized designation, so you will be assured of getting a competent planner, and by paying a flat hourly fee you will have piece of mind knowing your advisor is not pushing products due to financial incentive.

> The CFP designation is awarded by the CFP Board of Standards, an independent certifying body, upon successful completion of a 10-hour, two-day exam and three years of client experience (with bachelor's degree; five years without). You can get more information on CFPs and check out a CFP's status at *www.cfp.net*.

Choosing a financial planner is a very personal decision. In many ways it is as rife with complexities as choosing a mate, and equally expensive when it goes awry. Bill Mahoney, a fee-based financial planner located in Oxford, MA and president of the RISE Company, has the following to say about hiring a planner:

There is a great deal of discussion of why anyone needs a financial professional in their lives today. The main reason to hire a professional is the advice and education that you receive. Contrary to popular opinion, the vast majority of people can use a good financial professional in their lives.

A solid financial professional will do a lot more than just sell you a mutual fund or an insurance product. They will give you the basic information and education to help you make the financial decisions that affect your and your family's lives. Picking which mutual funds to use should be the last step.

What you should demand from a financial professional is that they get to know you and your financial life in detail, before they ever give you any advice or tell you to use a certain financial product. You should also demand that they give you some help in defining your financial goals, and how you are going to meet them.

In the area of investing, a good pro should give you the basic education you need to make an informed investment decision. They should educate you about what market caps are, what modern portfolio basics are, and the risks associated with the investments you are considering. The biggest job the pro has here is in helping you set the asset allocation of your different portfolios.

Resources

GARRETT PLANNING NETWORK

The Garret Planning Network is a group of fee-only advisors who charge for their services primarily by the hour. Visit their website at *www.garrettplanningnetwork.com*.

NAPFA

The National Association of Personal Financial Advisors is an organization made up of fee-only financial planners, the majority of whom are certified financial planners. The association's website is *www.napfa.com*.

You can check out a CFP's status at *www.cfp.net*, the website of the Certified Planner Board of Standards, an independent certifying body.

You can further investigate brokers and advisors through this link at the Securities and Exchange Commission: *www.sec.gov/investor/brokers.htm*.

Questions to ask a planner

It is strongly recommended that you interview at least three planners. The following questions should help in the process.

1. What is your educational background?
2. What is your financial planning education?
3. How long have you been offering financial services?
4. How many hours of continuing education do you take each year?
5. Have you ever been cited by a professional or regulatory body for disciplinary reasons?
6. Will I work with you directly?
7. What is your investment philosophy?
8. Please lay out all fees or commissions involved, including all costs of mutual funds or variable annuity sub accounts.
9. Do you put your recommendations in writing? (If not, walk away.)
10. Do you prepare my financial plan or does a computer?
11. How will the plan be implemented?
12. How often will we meet?
13. How are you compensated? Please disclose in detail.
14. Are you registered with the state or SEC (Securities Exchange Commission) as a Registered Investment Advisor? If so, may I see your form ADV part II? This disclosure document required by the SEC has information on the advisor's services, fees, and investment strategies.
15. Please explain diversification and why it is important.

How advisors are compensated

- *Commission* — Earns money by selling you a financial product.
- *Asset management fee* — Earns money through an annual fee based on percent of assets under management.
- *Hourly fee* — Earns money purely by the hour like an accountant or lawyer.
- *Fee-based* — Charges fees and commissions (combination of commission and asset management fees).

THE EIGHTH COMMANDMENT

Avoid credit card debt

One of the best investment you can make is paying off your entire credit card balances every month. It makes little sense to contribute to a retirement plan that you hope will earn 11 percent while you simultaneously pay 18 percent in finance charges on debt. If you have credit card debt, you are not alone. Misery may love company, but misery typically does not retire happy, healthy, and wise.

According to the annual Credit Card Survey conducted by Myvesta, a nonprofit consumer education organization, as of December 2004, the average American is now carrying $2,627 in credit card debt, up from $2,294 in 2003.

Before you even begin to think about contributing to a retirement plan, you should first pay off all credit card debt. This may not be what you want to hear, but hear it you must. Credit card debt is not only a drain on your personal finances; it is a drain on your personal well-being. Whether you admit it or not, debt can shape how you feel about yourself. Best-selling financial author Suze Orman contends that credit card debt contributes to the bottom line—as in extra body weight. She believes that when the debt goes down, the pounds come off.

If you have credit card debt, make a plan to pay it off before contributing to a retirement plan. Resist the temptation to make only the minimum payment. In fact, strive to pay at a minimum double or triple this amount. With discipline, you can eliminate credit card debt. The rewards will be enormous. Imagine contributing $500 a month for several years to pay down credit card debt. Once the debt is paid off, that $500 can then be directed to your retirement. As we learned in Chapter Five, if you pledge $500 a month to a tax-deferred savings plan, you will actually save $125 per month in taxes (assuming you are in the 25 percent marginal tax bracket). It is as if someone is suddenly paying you $125 monthly! Plus, your full $500 will be working for you each month instead of a credit card company.

Laura, a thirty-seven-year-old Maryland middle school teacher, and her husband eliminated $52,000 in debt in less than four years. She describes how:

> A few months before our wedding, I moved into my husband's house in a new state (Maryland). Since we had agreed that I would be the CFO [chief financial officer] of our family, one of my first tasks upon moving in was setting up the bill-paying desk. I knew my fiancé was a bit disorganized, but as I sorted through his papers, I discovered to my horror that he had more than $21,000 in credit card debt! I was angry that he had not told me and worried that there might be more. I was also confused as to why he had not told me. After I confronted him, I made him show me all debt. In addition to

the $21,000 credit card liability, there was $35,000 in student loan debt, a $12,000 car loan, and a $173,000 mortgage. I had $14,000 in student loan debt myself, putting our total debt at $255,000. I focused on the debt, not my horror, and came up with a plan. Here is what worked for us.

1. *Stop the bleeding*

   I discovered my husband had been paying huge late fees because he did not have a system for organizing and paying bills on time. My system: I put all invoices in an "outgoing mail" rack marked by date due. I then filed each statement by company name. Simply paying the bills on time saved us hundreds of dollars a month.

2. *Pay the lowest interest rate you can*

   First, I prioritized our credit card debt by interest rate. I paid the minimum on the credit cards with lower rates and put any extra cash I had into the higher rate accounts. I also looked for deals to lower the rates. EXAMPLE: One of the lines of credit sent these special checks with 4.9 percent interest for six months. I immediately wrote a check for the balance on one of the cards charging 20% interest. Then, about four months later, we got an offer in the mail for zero interest on balance transfers for four months, so I transferred the balance from another one of the 20 percent cards there. I had to be very careful to either pay off the transferred balances by the end of the grace period or find another card to switch them to, but the effort saved us hundreds of dollars a month.

3. *Other financial moves*

   For simplicity I consolidated our student loans with the U.S. Department of Education. When my husband's income rose, we refinanced to a fifteen-year mortgage, which has helped us accumulate equity much faster. We also moved our car loan to a tax-deductible home-equity line of credit. We switched to credit unions, which paid a higher interest rate on our savings and charged less in monthly fees.

4. *Change spending habits*

   My husband had accumulated a lot of debt wooing me—nice dinners, long-distance phone calls, and so forth. While we did not totally kill the romance, we tried to limit our nights out to cheaper ethnic restaurants. It helps that I like to shop at estate sales for furniture and secondhand stores for clothes. Plus, we volunteer at a local concert series and in exchange get to see the concerts for free. My goal for our money: one-third for Uncle Sam, one-third for savings, and one-third to spend.

5. *Save even when it hurts*

   I contribute the maximum amount to a 403(b) plan ($14,000 for year 2005). This is about 20 percent of my pay. Once we paid off our credit card debt, we started to put all of my salary (after the 403(b) deduction) into regular savings. Then, when tax time comes, we apply any refund to our debts. Additionally, my husband participates in a retirement plan at work. He works in a very cyclical industry; he has been out of a job four times in five years, so there are times we cannot save, but whenever he is working, we are saving.

6. *Do not be proud*

When we moved to the Washington, DC area, which is very expensive, we found that the house we wanted cost more than we could afford. We took in a roommate, who writes the "rent" checks straight to our student loans, so we never see the money as income that we might spend.

7. *Track the progress*

I have a folder called "Debt Profile," which I update regularly. What does our profile say now?

- $21,000 in credit card debt: gone
- Student loan debt: down to $18,000 from $49,000
- Overall net worth: up $275,000 in seven years

THE NINTH COMMANDMENT
Take the long view

The retirement plans outlined in this book are for retirement, which for most of us is a long time off. Investing in stock mutual funds can be a very volatile, hence risky, endeavor in the short term (meaning they are held less than five years). Unfortunately, studies show that investors have very little patience for market volatility. A recent report from Dalbar, Inc., a provider of financial research, revealed that from 1984 to 2003 the average investor earned a paltry 2.57 percent annually. When inflation (3.14 percent annually) is factored in, investors actually lost money. These results contrast sharply with the 12.22 percent that the S&P 500 returned during that same period (before inflation, fees, and taxes). Why the disparity in performance? During the periods when the market declined between 1984 and 2003 many investors pulled their money out of stocks and went into bonds. When bonds declined and stocks soared, investors who had pulled out of stocks were unable to participate in the rebound. This meant that many investors had lost twice in one market cycle. History tells us that investors who properly allocate investments and take a long-term perspective have the best chance of realizing their retirement goals.

THE TENTH COMMANDMENT
Have your entire financial house in order

The 403(b), the 457(b), and the Roth IRA accounts are amazing wealth-building tools. But as important as these are, they are merely one part of your overall financial plan. Other questions demand your attention. Do you have enough insurance—life, disability, long-term care, property, casualty, auto, and so on? Do you have a Will, trust, and Power of Attorney? The wisest course of action may be to first take care of these tasks (explained in Chapter Five) before embarking on a 403(b), 457(b), or Roth IRA.

CHAPTER TWELVE

D-I-V-O-R-C-E Can Spell Financial Disaster

"Caution is the eldest child of wisdom." — Victor Hugo

> The latest information from the National Center for Health Statistics reveals that for every two marriages in 2003 there was one divorce.

While the three first letters in divorce (d-i-v) might lead one to believe that such a parting always results in an equal "d-i-v"-ision of assets, such an assumption would be wrong. Why discuss something as negative as divorce in a book like this? There are many reasons, including the following.

1. Divorce can be financially devastating to everyone involved.
2. Divorce is unfortunately all too common, even among teachers.
3. Divorce can thrust many into the difficult position of having to manage money for the very first time.
4. Divorce can result in an unequal division of assets.
5. Divorce tends to have a more adverse financial effect on women than on men. According to the NEA, nearly 80 percent of public school teachers are women.

Since 1981, the ratio of male teachers to female teachers has steadily declined. In 2003, says the NEA, it stood at a forty-year low of one male teacher for every four female teachers.

Scott Dauenhauer, CFP, is a fee-only financial planner and owner of Meridian Wealth Management. He specializes in working with teachers. He recounts his experience with teachers and divorce here:

A surprisingly large number of my clients are divorced teachers. Interestingly, most of these are women. While their situations are all unique, they generally share the following characteristics:

1. They have never managed personal finances.
2. They are not comfortable with budgeting, planning, or investing.
3. They have a strong desire to be financially independent and knowledgeable.

Again, these are general observations from my experience. I realize that no two people, situations, or divorces are exactly the same. I can say, however, that anyone who is contemplating divorce, gone through a divorce, or is thinking about remarrying should seriously consider speaking with a financial professional.

The most important advice I can give someone going through a divorce is to get your own representation. Going further, I would recommend that you work with a qualified financial advisor who can help you judge the fairness of any proposed settlement. You may think that it is your attorney's job to ensure you get a fair settlement (and it is), but many attorneys are not well-versed in tax law, pension systems, insurance, Social Security, and other retirement issues that are unique to teachers. Each of these areas needs to be examined closely for your protection. Retirement plan rules vary by state and can be quite complex. Using a planner should not be construed as a slap in the face of your attorney. On the contrary, your lawyer should welcome working with a financial advisor—unless, of course, he or she is very experienced in teacher retirement plans and the tax code. You may well be concerned about the cost of hiring a planner in addition to an attorney. This is a very valid concern, but let me tell you a story that is all too possible.

131

"Susan," a teacher, is about to make her divorce final. Her soon-to-be ex-husband proposes to give Susan his retirement account (valued at approximately $100,000) in exchange for her giving up all rights to a second housing property. The property was jointly purchased and is valued at approximately $100,000.

On the surface this sounds like a fair exchange, but the proposal actually has the potential to be extremely biased—against Susan. Why? Taxes. If Susan agrees to the exchange and taps the retirement account, her withdrawals would be fully taxable. She is not required to draw this money right away, but what if she needs the money for living expenses? Approximately 25 percent to 30 percent of any withdrawal would be lost to taxes.

The residential property, on the other hand, would be taxable only at the capital-gains rate of 15 percent. If Susan's ex-husband takes up residence in the property for two years, he would be able to avoid capital-gains taxes altogether. Plus, the real estate has a chance to significantly appreciate in value.

Susan's story is just one potential financial pitfall that could beset someone during a divorce. A myriad of even more expensive traps loom. For that reason, I urge you to seek both legal and financial counsel.

The ramifications of divorce on 403(b) and 457(b) plans are covered in Chapter Five.

CHAPTER THIRTEEN

Tax Savings on Classroom, Health Care, and Dependent Care Expenses

"The wages of sin are death, but by the time taxes are taken out, it's just sort of a tired feeling." — Paula Poundstone

This book has already highlighted the tax benefits of participating in various retirement plans (Chapter Five). But what about the countless out-of-pocket dollars that teachers spend on their classrooms? What about health care expenses not covered by insurance? And what about dependent care expenses?

OUT-OF-POCKET CLASSROOM EXPENSES

It has been estimated that teachers spend more than $520 each per year in out-of-pocket expenses on their classrooms. First-year teachers reportedly spend more than $700 each. Recognizing this financial burden, Congress passed the Teacher Tax Relief Act of 2001, which allows teachers to deduct up to $250 of classroom expenses. Many states also offer special tax relief to teachers. Furthermore, the cost of course work for career advancement is typically always deductible—as is the travel mileage for doing the course work. It should be noted that teachers are not eligible to deduct mileage traveled to and from work, but they may deduct mileage for work-related travel from school—travel from the teacher's school to a meeting at the district office or another school, for instance. Track all of these expenses so you can deduct them at tax time.

HEALTH CARE AND DEPENDENT CARE EXPENSES
Flexible Spending Account (FSA)

These plans allow employees to set aside a specified dollar amount from their gross pay (pre-tax) to pay for out-of-pocket health care and dependent care expenses. FSAs are one of the most overlooked benefits available to employees. According to WageWorks, which provides FSA health care and dependent care spending accounts for large employers, only about 12 percent of eligible employees participate in these accounts. FSAs allow individuals to set aside money through a special payroll deduction. This means that FSA contributions are usually exempt from state and federal taxes. Withdrawals for health care and dependent care expenses are made tax-free.

The major drawback to the FSA is that all money in the account must be used in the year in which it is contributed. This means that individuals can find themselves scrambling in December to draw down their accounts. It makes you wonder why the word flexible is part of the name of the plan, doesn't it? But do not let this discourage you from investing in these accounts. Setting aside even $500 could result in a savings of $150 in taxes. In effect, you would need to spend only $350 to break even. While life is fraught with uncertainty, especially when it comes to health care issues, a little health care and dependent care preplanning could result in some significant tax savings.

Health Care FSA

Under current rules (2005), up to $4,000 can be set aside for health care expenses. What follows, from WageWorks and

Bankrate.com, is a list of some of the major health care expenses that can be paid with FSA money.

- Co-payments and deductibles
- Orthodontia
- Dental
- Prescription drugs
- Over-the-counter drugs
- Prescription eyeglasses and sunglasses
- Contact lenses and solutions
- Laser eye surgery
- Chiropractic care
- Counseling or therapy
- Fertility treatments and procedures
- Acupuncture
- Birth control

Dependent Care FSA

If you are single, or married and file jointly, you may set aside up to $5,000 in an FSA for dependent care expenses in 2005. If you are married and file separately, you may save up to $2,500. What follows is a list from WageWorks of some of the dependent care expenses eligible to be paid with FSA money.

- Adult day-care centers
- Babysitting
- Before- and after-school programs
- Child care
- Elder care
- Preschool

- Senior day care
- Sick child care
- Summer day camp

Your employer may offer a Health Care FSA, a Dependent Care FSA, or both. Since each category is separate, you must specify which account(s) you want. Contact your employer for more information about setting up an FSA account. Unions often negotiate this benefit for their members. An FSA must be set up through an employer. Individuals are not able to set up their own FSA accounts.

Health Savings Account (HSA)

Congress recently created the Health Savings Account (HSA), which allows participants to pay for current health expenses and save for future qualified medical and retiree health expenses on a tax-free basis. The advantage of the HSA over the FSA is that individuals can set up their own accounts (generally through insurance companies and banks), and money not used can carry over to future years. According to the United States Department of Treasury, to be eligible for an HSA, a participant must be covered by a High Deductible Health Plan (HDHP), must not be covered by other health insurance (does not apply to insurance for specific injuries or accidents, disability, dental care, vision care, and long-term care), is not eligible for Medicare, and cannot be claimed as a dependent on someone else's tax return. Under current rules (2005), an HDHP is a health insurance plan with a minimum deductible of $1,000 (single participant) or $2,000 (family). The nascent HSA may very well be the future of how individuals, families and employers pay for health care coverage. The reason? The hope is that if individuals have a financial stake or "ownership" in their health care plan they will manage it more cost-effectively, thus reducing health care costs. The reward for the individual is an HSA balance that could grow annually. The fear? Not enough Americans will understand it, participate in it, or be able to afford it. Expect to see and hear much more about HSAs in the coming years. For complete details on the HSA visit the United States Department of Treasury website at *www.treas.gov*.

HOMEWORK: Check with your employer to see if a Flexible Spending Account plan is offered. If it is not offered, request that one be added. You may also want to see if your union would consider negotiating the inclusion of an FSA plan. Research the new Health Savings Account at the United States Department of Treasury website (*www.treas.gov*). In the search box on the home page, type in "Health Savings Accounts."

CHAPTER FOURTEEN

Managing Money in Retirement

"I have enough money to last me the rest of my life, unless I buy something." — Jackie Mason

A quick review of asset allocation from Chapter Eight: as you approach retirement, your portfolio should be more weighted toward fixed investments than stocks. If you have chosen a target-date fund, this will have been done automatically for you. If you have wisely allocated your investments as you approach retirement, you can rest easy knowing that a sudden market drop will not adversely affect your plans. Sadly, many teachers on the cusp of retirement in the years 1999–2002 were not properly allocated and paid the price when the bottom fell out of the market. In fact, many may still be working today trying to recoup their losses.

Some may feel comfortable in retirement only if they are 100 percent invested in fixed investments. That is fine if one understands that the ravages of inflation result in a gradual increase in the cost of living. The round of golf that costs $24 the day you retire may cost $36 five years later. Can your investments absorb this kind of cost increase?

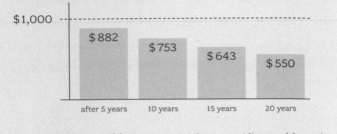

THE INFLATION GAP

This chart illustrates the declining purchasing power of $1,000 over time, using a 3.1% annual inflation rate. After 20 years, the $1,000 only buys what $550 bought in the first year of retirement.

$1,000

$882 — after 5 years
$753 — 10 years
$643 — 15 years
$550 — 20 years

SOURCE: Meridian Wealth Management (*www.meridianwealth.com*).

Even in retirement, it is important that some of your portfolio be dedicated to stocks. Why? Recall from Chapter Eight that stocks and stock funds participate in profits, while bonds and fixed investments do not. This means that stocks and stock funds have the ability to grow and counter the effects of inflation. Fixed investments, on the other hand, will steady your portfolio when the market declines, but they cannot fully benefit when the market goes up. They simply do not capture the full effect of the market's rise. Target-date funds take this into consideration and maintain a stock presence even after the target retirement date has been reached.

It is also important to understand that retirement is not an end. It is actually a beginning. The beginning of a new phase of your life that demographers tell us could last for decades. That's good news for retirees and their golf game—especially if they have saved, allocated wisely, and are deft on the putting green.

But it becomes imperative that you also factor an increase in life expectancy into how much you need to save.

LIFE EXPECTANCY

It has been estimated that most retirees will live at least 20 years in retirement. It is interesting to note that during the 20th century, life expectancy at birth increased from 48 to 74 years of age for men and from 51 to almost 80 years of age for women.*

> **HOMEWORK:** Do a web search for "life expectancy calculators." Input your specific information into a suitable calculator to determine your life expectancy.

RETIREMENT MANAGEMENT WARNING

Several retirement strategies and tips will be outlined here. Since every individual has his or her own needs and demands, it would be unwise for anyone to rely solely on the points made here. Numerous complex rules govern the withdrawal of retirement money. For that reason alone, consulting a financial advisor makes enormous sense (recall the section on seeking wise financial counsel from Chapter Eleven). Furthermore, it is critical that your retirement strategy be designed to ensure that you do not run out of money in retirement. This may sound beyond obvious. It is, but increased life expectancy and the effects of inflation make lifetime liquidity difficult to achieve. This is not to say that you cannot successfully manage all aspects of your

* SOURCE: *Health, United States, 2004*, a report from Centers for Disease Control and Prevention (CDC).

own retirement, but $500 to $5,000 spent plotting a retirement strategy with the assistance of a reputable financial planner may be your best investment of all.

Questions to ask yourself as you plan your retirement
QUESTION ONE: *How much do you need to live on? Planners call this "creating a vision."*

This question can be difficult to answer. On one hand, you may have paid off your house, thus reducing a major expense. On the other hand, you might find that all the free time retirement affords to be quite expensive. Luckily, most teachers have had a glimpse of retirement (also called summer vacation!) and have had the experience of budgeting accordingly. Financial planners recommend that you strive to have sufficient savings to replace 70 percent to 90 percent of your pre-retirement income. EXAMPLE: If in your last year of teaching you earned $50,000, you would need an annual income of $35,000 in retirement to reach the minimum 70 percent target. This is assuming, of course, that you can live on a reduced income—in this case 30 percent, or $15,000, less. Do not forget, also, that $35,000 today will be worth far less tomorrow. You will have to increase your withdrawal amount annually just to keep pace with inflation.

QUESTION TWO: *How much income will your defined-benefit plan and/or Social Security provide?*

If you are fortunate enough to have a defined-benefit plan (as described in Chapter Five) and to have taught for twenty-five to thirty-five years, you can probably count on replacing 50 percent to 70 percent of your pre-retirement income. Upon retirement, these plans typically promise an income for life, based on years of service and a retirement factor determined by each state. For specific rules applicable to your situation, contact the state agency that operates your plan. Recall from Chapter Five that it is wise to become familiar with the exact workings of your DB plan years before you actually retire. Some of you may even be eligible to draw Social Security in addition to a pension. As we all know, the future of Social Security is tenuous at best. Assume nothing as it relates to Social Security. Plus, rules such as the Government Pension Offset (GPO) and the Windfall Elimination Provision (WEP) penalize teachers who draw from a non-Social Security pension plan and from Social Security.

> To find out if and how GPO and WEP rules apply to you, contact the Social Security Administration. You can visit a local office or go to *www.ssa.gov* website. The National Education Association website (*www.nea.org*) also has information on these provisions. A competent financial planner should be able to provide you with the exact rules relevant to your situation.

The good news about DB plans and Social Security is that they typically are adjusted for inflation. Arguments can be made about whether or not the adjustment is sufficient, but most plans do something.

Generally, you can expect to draw from your DB plan a retirement factor (generally around 2 percent) multiplied by the number of years worked multiplied by the average of your three highest paid years. EXAMPLE: Twenty-five years worked multiplied by 2 percent entitles you to 50 percent of the average of your three highest-paid years. Let's assume the average of your three highest-paid years is $50,000. This means you will be able to draw 50 percent of this amount, or $25,000, annually. As we go to Question Three lets assume you are able to draw $25,000 annually from some combination of your DB plan and Social Security.

You can determine your projected Social Security payout by visiting *www.ssa.gov*. If you do not have a DB plan, chances are that your payout from Social Security will fall short of replacing 70 percent of your pre-retirement income. A shortfall means you will need to save and draw much more from your 403(b), 457(b), or Roth IRA or from other savings to reach 70 percent to 90 percent of your pre-retirement income.

QUESTION THREE: *Should you convert some of your retirement plans' principal into a steady income (immediate annuity) or should you gradually draw down your investments (systematic withdrawal)?*

In an ideal retirement scenario you would draw 70 percent or more of your pre-retirement income from some combination of your DB plan and Social Security. Some teachers are fortunate enough to be in such a situation. If this describes you, it would be wise to avoid touching your 403(b), 457(b), or Roth IRA for as long as possible. The reason? Since money in these plans enjoys tax-free growth, let them grow, let them grow, let them grow! Plus, drawing on these funds in addition to a pension may increase your tax obligation.

For this next exercise let us continue our previous assumption that your goal is to replace 70 percent of your pre-retirement income, which was $50,000. This means that you need to draw $35,000 annually (70 percent of $50,000) from some combination of your savings plans. Let us further assume that you will receive $25,000 annually from some combination of your DB plan and Social Security. How can you make up that last $10,000?

Let us also assume you have wisely squirreled away $250,000 in some combination of 403(b) and 457(b) plans. Aren't you glad you started saving in these plans? Don't you wish you had begun earlier, contributed more, and been invested in low-cost funds earlier? It is easy to play the would-have, should-have game. Just be glad you got wise to these plans at some point!

For simplicity's sake, it may make sense, once you have retired, to move the balance of both the 403(b) and 457(b) into a rollover IRA (rules are different than a Roth IRA). This way all of your money is held in one account, making management simpler (you can review how to move your money into a rollover IRA in Chapter Five). An added bonus of this maneuver is that you are free to move the money to the financial institution of your choice. This is of particular value to teachers who did not have access to quality vendors while working. You are, of course, free to leave your 403(b) or 457(b) money where it is if you are happy with your plan.

Your next decision is to determine how you wish to draw money from your account(s). There are two main ways to withdraw money in retirement: annuitiziation and systematic withdrawal plan.

WITHDRAWAL OPTION ONE: ANNUITIZE ALL OR SOME PORTION OF BALANCE TO ENSURE REGULAR GUARANTEED PAYOUTS

With annuitization, you are basically trading all or a portion of your principal for a guaranteed stream of payments. A variety of annuitizing plans exist. A few will be explained here.

- You can annuitize over the length of your life (lifetime annuity) and receive monthly, quarterly, or annual payments. The payments can be fixed or variable and will cease upon your death whether you live forty-five years or just more six months.

- To ensure the protection of loved ones in the event of your early death, you can annuitize over your life and that of another (joint life expectancy or two-life annuity). In this case, payments cease upon the death of the second person. In order to account for the probability of one or both people living longer, payments are smaller.

- You can also annuitize for a set number of years, usually five or more, and can include just yourself, or yourself and a loved one.

In January 2005, the website *immediateannuity.com* showed the following information for a healthy sixty-three-year-old male living in Texas:

- In exchange for $132,384, this individual will receive $833 monthly for life. This would achieve the goal of drawing $10,000 annually. Payment would cease upon death.
- In exchange for $133,327, this individual will receive $833 monthly for life with a five-year guarantee. If he dies during the first five years of this agreement, his beneficiaries will receive the monthly stipend through the end of the fifth year.
- In exchange for $140,323, this individual will receive the same $833 monthly payout with a fifteen-year guarantee. Ten- and twenty-year guarantees also exist.
- In exchange for $160,131, this individual can guarantee $833 a month for life for himself and his sixty-one-year-old wife. Payment ceases upon the death of the second person.

The advantage of annuitizing is that you are guaranteed a steady income for life. The disadvantage is that you lose access to some portion or all of your principal.

Annuitizing is basically a bet that you are going to live longer than the insurance company thinks you will. If you do live longer, you benefit. If you do not, the company benefits. It should be pointed out that insurance companies are quite astute at estimating length of life and factoring their risk in payments.

HOMEWORK: Visit *www.immediateannuity.com* and try your hand with the annuity calculator. You can determine a payout for the amount of money that you have to invest or for the amount you need each month. You can calculate for male or female, single or married, state of residence, and so on.

WITHDRAWAL OPTION TWO: GRADUALLY DRAW DOWN YOUR
BALANCE THROUGH SYSTEMATIC WITHDRAWALS

Under such a plan you allocate your investments according to
your risk tolerance and then begin making withdrawals, usually on
a monthly or quarterly basis, or according to any other schedule
you desire.

- Numerous studies have shown that you can withdraw 4
  percent a year (inflation-adjusted) from a portfolio that is
  weighted 60 percent stock and 40 percent fixed investments
  and enjoy a high probability that you will not run out of
  money within thirty years.
- A balance of $250,000 withdrawn at a rate of 4 percent
  annually would yield the $10,000 you need for our example.

The advantages of a systematic withdrawal plan are that you
maintain access to your balance, retain flexibility, and have the
potential to pass the money to your heirs. The drawback is that
there is a possibility that you may outlive your money.

A wise idea is to set up a separate, safe account and fund it
with enough money to cover your living expenses for one
to three years. Draw from this account during a market
downturn. This way you are not liquidating other assets
during a market retreat (the worst time to sell).

Clearly, retiring on $35,000 a year will not catapult you into the ranks of the rich. But three points are to be made.

1. Those who start early and save regularly should be able to retire with the ability to draw considerably more money than $35,000 a year.

2. Our example focused only on an individual and did not factor in the retirement benefits available to a spouse.

3. The $35,000 figure was used as a baseline. This amount will make sense for some; for others it will not. You will need to gauge your own situation and save accordingly. If $35,000 seems to be inadequate, perhaps it will encourage you to save more now.

HOMEWORK: Three Trinity University professors—Philip L. Cooley, Carl M. Hubbard, and Daniel T. Walz—conducted one of the original studies on withdrawal rates. Their respected work is often referred to as the Trinity Study. Go to *www.google.com* and search "The Trinity Study." Read several of the relevant results and share them with at least two of your colleagues.

Conclusion

Thank you for spending time with this book. If you are new to investing this may all seem very daunting. It is not. I can tell you for certain it is nowhere near as difficult and challenging as facing a classroom of students each and every day. Just as no child learns to read or write on his or her first attempt, no teacher should expect to become an investment expert overnight. Begin slowly. Learn from and lean on colleagues. Keep in mind that saving for an arbitrary date in the future goes against human nature. That is why I write about "forced savings" and "automatic contributions." As humans, we have to literally will ourselves to save. Plus we live in a country where despite all that is written about saving, not a whole lot of it is going on. The U.S. is truly a country of disparate savers. Half of all households accumulate some savings, while the other half save nothing, according to a TIAA-CREF Institute research report "Do We Have a Retirement Crisis in America?"

I suppose the best analogy I can draw to show the similarity between saving and teaching is summer vacation. Most of us have experienced the joy that is summer vacation. It is a time of blissful freedom—if, of course, you have set aside enough money to fully enjoy it. Retirement is truly permanent summer vacation. To ensure the sunniest and most enjoyable retirement, you have to plan accordingly. It just takes a little forethought and, yes, forced savings! Begin now. Even if you can only save a little bit. Contribute to your savings regularly because time is on your side. Pay attention to asset allocation and pay attention to fees. You can do this. Class dismissed!

My approach to saving for retirement

I am often asked about my approach to saving for retirement.
The best answer is that it is a work in progress. I have always paid
attention to fees and asset allocation, and I have always strived to
contribute as much as possible to my retirement plans. But as far
as the individual investments I own for retirement, I have shifted
from a holder of numerous index and managed mutual funds to a
retirement portfolio almost exclusively invested in one low-cost
target-date fund.

I first became a fan of this approach in 1998 when I was
arranging a 529 college savings plan for our daughter. California,
our state at the time, called the approach age-based allocation.
I was immediately attracted to the simplicity of it all, not to
mention the low fees in the non-broker plan. I loved the fact that
asset allocation automatically shifted to a more conservative
investment mix as college age approached. All I had to do was
make regular contributions to one fund. I laughed at the thought
of Lily becoming more bold and aggressive (teenage years) as her
college investments are becoming more conservative. This got me
to thinking... how can I get Lily's behavior to mirror her portfolio?
Now that would a challenge! I think I would have a better chance
of beating the market with a high-fee variable annuity! But
seriously, this experience made me think about my approach to
saving for retirement.

Why should I spend countless hours rearranging my own
retirement portfolio to ensure proper asset allocation when I
can pick one low-cost target-date fund and let the efficiency of
the market over time build a comfortable nest egg? Some argue

that the target retirement date approach is geared toward a broad segment of investors and does not take individual needs into account. True enough. Agents and brokers love to tout their investment picking prowess, their program trading techniques, and their computer-based investment models. Funny how they never tout their fees and the fact that the overwhelming majority of managed funds fail to beat the market, and that those that do are usually unable to sustain performance over time. For my money, I have simply read too much from the wise minds of William Bernstein, John C. Bogle, Burton G. Malkiel and Warren Buffett to believe that so-called financial experts—who are often younger than I am—can successfully beat the market over time when all expenses are factored in.

This is not to say that I do not believe in the services of financial professionals. On the contrary, I often consult a superb hourly fee financial planner (thanks, Scott Dauenhauer, CFP) and a sage accountant (thanks, Doug Brentlinger, CPA) for many of my individual money management questions. Their advice and counsel has already yielded an impressive return. I have employed the services of a terrific attorney (thanks, George Atkinson) to draft a living trust, Will, and Power of Attorney. My wife and I update this document regularly. As retirement approaches I will only lean on these individuals more.

I hold investments outside of retirement including a few individual stocks and a few select low-fee index mutual funds in sectors I see enormous long-term potential: real estate investment trusts (REIT) and the health care industry. Because my core retirement holdings are properly allocated in one low-cost target-date fund focused on the long term, I am comfortable investing other money in select securities I deem of value.

In short, I truly believe that I practice what I have preached in this book. Actually, I hope I have not preached, but have instead taught. Each of us is unique with our own unique needs. My approach to retirement works for my situation. I encourage you to craft an approach that works for yours.

Appendix

Recommended reading

- *9 Steps to Financial Freedom: Practical and Spiritual Steps So You Can Stop Worrying* by Suze Orman — An interesting look at how views of money are often shaped by family history. Excellent primer for overall financial education including the necessity of a Will, trust, Power of Attorney, and insurance. (ISBN 0-609-80186-4)

- *The Average Family's Guide to Financial Freedom* by Bill and Mary Toohey — Learn how this Iowa couple saved a small fortune ($500,000), paid off their mortgage, and achieved an enviable work-to-leisure-time ratio all on a modest annual income ($65,000), while raising three kids, one of whom has a severe disability. (ISBN 0-471-35228-4)

- *The Two-Income Trap: Why Middle-Class Mothers and Fathers Are Going Broke* by Elizabeth Warren and Amelia Warren Tyagi — Eye-opening reading on the financial demands of families, and the predatory practices of the credit card industry. (ISBN 0-465-09082-6)

- *Who Moved My Cheese? An Amazing Way to Deal with Change in Your Work and in Your Life* by Spencer Johnson, M.D. — How to cope with change in a fast-changing world; especially valuable as we move to an "ownership society" requiring individuals to be directly responsible for their financial future. (ISBN 0-399-14446-3)

- *Common Sense on Mutual Funds: New Imperatives for the Intelligent Investor* by John C. Bogle — Investors owe an enormous debt of gratitude to the former chairman of Vanguard and father of the index fund for his commitment to low-fees and investor rights, among many other public-minded pursuits. His book makes a strong case for the index approach to investing. (ISBN 0-471-39228-6)

- *The Four Pillars of Investing: Lessons for Building a Winning Portfolio* by William Bernstein — Interesting history on the markets and the psychology of investing coupled with practical advice on building a portfolio. Mr. Bernstein also explains why much of the mutual fund and brokerage instustries "instead of being your partners, are often your most direct competitors." (ISBN 0-071-38529-0)

- *A Random Walk Down Wall Street* by Burton G. Malkiel — Author's 1973 thesis that "investors would be far better off buying and holding an index fund than attempting to buy and sell individual securities or actively managed mutual funds" remains sound today. Updated edition contains lessons from the great technology bust of 2000 and model life-cycle portfolios to keep investors in proper asset allocation every step of their investing lives. (ISBN 0-393-32535-0)

- *The Late Start Investor: The Better-Late-Than-Never Guide to Realizing Your Retirement Dreams* by John F. Wasik — Provides hope for investors 50 and over who have saved very little toward retirement. (ISBN 0-805-05502-9)

- *Marv Levy: Where Else Would You Rather Be?* by Marv Levy —

Sorry, but I am hopelessly hooked on Buffalo Bills football. This book by the Bills' Hall-of-Fame coach will teach you virtually nothing about money management, but instead tells the story of an amazing teacher over a 47-year coaching odyssey. The book is peppered with stirring quotes Mr. Levy used to teach and inspire: "What you do speaks so loudly no one can hear what you are saying," "Adversity is an opportunity for heroism," and "Expect rejection, but expect more to overcome it." (ISBN 1-582-61797-X)

Where to get your questions answered

No single book can answer all of your financial questions. Rules and laws governing retirement plans are constantly changing. A great place to get questions answered is the discussion board on the 403(b)wise website (*www.403bwise.com*).

For the latest investing news affecting teachers

Visit *www.teachandretirerich.com*, *www.403bwise.com*, and *www.457bwise.com*.

For updates to Teach and Retire Rich

Visit *www.teachandretirerich.com*.

Meet the author

If you are interested in information on having Dan Otter visit your school or organization to discuss concepts from this book, or if you have questions or comments for Dan, email him at *dan@teachandretirerich.com*.

Bulk order discounts

For information on receiving a discount on an order of five or more books, send an email to *bookorders@teachandretirerich.com*. Please state the number of books you are interested in purchasing.

Acknowledgements and Special Thanks

This book would never have been possible without all the special teachers in my life.

It is easy to thank most people for their enormous help with this book. It is nearly impossible to truly express my gratitude toward my wife, Mandy, for her contributions—laying out the book and correcting my often poorly constructed prose. Mandy is an award-winning designer at Threespot Media who has designed websites for the Peace Corps, Zipcar, and the National Museum of American History to name only a few. I literally have no idea how she was able to juggle *Teach and Retire Rich* with the demands of her career and our two children, including "little" Ben who arrived during this project. It is thanks to her sage stewardship that the title did not become *Teach and Go Crazy Trying to Raise a Family and Write a Book*.

Thank you Mom, Dad, Julie, Lily, Ben, Steve, Heather, and Mack for teaching me the meaning of love and support. Thank you Dad for teaching me at a young age the power of wise money management. Thank you John C. Bogle for teaching everyone that fees matter.

Thank you Carolyn Widener for the inspiration. Thank you Bill Bernstein for you wonderful foreward. Thank you Michael Devault and Scott Dauenhauer for your insightful proofing and content suggestions. Thank you John D'Antonio for your astute editing.

Thank you Mr. Rodriguez for making U.S. History so exciting. Thank you Mrs. Irons for providing me plenty of rope in my creative efforts.

Thank you Brian Cressey for your unwavering support of 403(b)wise. Thank you to the hundreds of thousands of visitors who have made 403(b)wise such a popular website. And thank you again to the 403(b) warriors: Steve Schullo, Ted Leber, Bill Mahoney, Adrian Nenu, Gary Turbak, Joel L. Frank, Chuck Yanikoski, Joe MacDonald, and G. Wade Caldwell.

ABOUT THE AUTHOR

DAN OTTER is a father, husband, teacher, author, and operator of two websites that are designed to educate and empower, *www.403bwise.com* and *www.457bwise.com*. He also creates customized retirement plan information websites for school districts (*www.yourplan.info*). He has taught grades one, three, four, five, six and at the college level. Dan's first book, *The 403(b) Wise Guide*, which he co-wrote with planner Scott Dauenhauer, sold more than 10,000 copies and was described by John C. Bogle as "right on!" Dan has appeared on National Public Radio and has written on retirement issues for the Motley Fool website. He also speaks to schools and other organizations about the *Teach and Retire Rich* concepts outlined in this book.